D1287928

RHYTHMS OF CHANGE IN ROCKY MOUNTAIN NATIONAL PARK

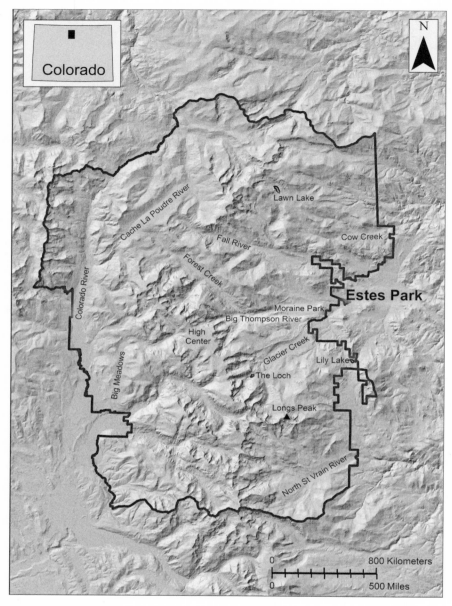

Rocky Mountain National Park. Courtesy of Annette Patton.

Rhythms of Change in Rocky Mountain National Park

ELLEN WOHL

UNIVERSITY PRESS OF KANSAS

© 2016 by the University Press of Kansas
All rights reserved

Published by the University Press of Kansas (Lawrence, Kansas 66045), which was
organized by the Kansas Board of Regents and is operated and funded by Emporia
State University, Fort Hays State University, Kansas State University, Pittsburg State
University, the University of Kansas, and Wichita State University

Library of Congress Cataloging-in-Publication Data

Names: Wohl, Ellen E., 1962–
Title: Rhythms of change in Rocky Mountain National Park / Ellen Wohl.
Description: Lawrence : University Press of Kansas, [2016] | Includes bibliographical
references and index.
Identifiers: LCCN 2016028702
ISBN 9780700623365 (cloth : alk. paper)
ISBN 9780700623372 (ebook)
Subjects: LCSH: Natural history—Colorado—Rocky Mountain National Park. |
Seasons—Colorado—Rocky Mountain National Park. | Geology—Colorado—
Rocky Mountain National Park. | Landscape changes—Colorado—Rocky Mountain
National Park. | Rocky Mountain National Park (Colo.)
Classification: LCC QH105.C6 W645 2016 | DDC 508.788/69—dc23
LC record available at https://lccn.loc.gov/2016028702.

British Library Cataloguing-in-Publication Data is available.

Printed in the United States of America

10 9 8 7 6 5 4 3 2 1

The paper used in this publication is recycled and contains 30 percent postconsumer
waste. It is acid free and meets the minimum requirements of the American National
Standard for Permanence of Paper for Printed Library Materials Z39.48-1992.

Contents

Usually, time slides by us as water ripples away from a small boat, a kayak or canoe slipping quietly across the reflected sky. Often we don't notice. Or else subtle waves mark its passing, a pattern of soft hills and dips you want to feel beneath your palm, even though you know that touching them will change them.

But once in a while, minutes pool into moments of particular intensity and meaning. Rarely, these are the personal earthquakes that dramatically change the ways we inhabit and understand the world. More often, they are what the poet Wordsworth called "spots of time," quiet moments in which "our minds / Are nourished and invisibly repaired." Mostly we have only to recognize them as they come, unbidden. Or with no guarantees that they will arrive, we can invite them and make ourselves ready.

And so I am standing here alone waiting for the sun to rise on New Year's Day.

As a magical gesture of hope for the shape of the year to come, I like to spend this holiday doing something I love, and often this means being in the mountains. Even the most arbitrary cultural markers carry meaning, and this one, the day for new beginnings, also marks the depth of winter in my half of the globe, that space between the shortest and the coldest days. I have chosen this spot on Trail Ridge Road—Many Parks Curve, just where the road is closed for the winter—because I know it offers a good view to the east. My husband, John, dozes in the car behind my back, giving me this solitary time outdoors.

I had hoped for a brilliant sunrise, the silvery glow of midwinter flooding over the valley and peaks. But I know now I won't see the sun enter the day, any more than I will see the new moon appear just a few minutes earlier. A thick layer of white hides the horizon. And I am wrapped in a mountain cloud. Snowflakes swirl around me, lost against the matching sky, soft white against the dark needles and bark of the trees. The moist air itself dances a ghostly dance, obscuring nearly everything, then offering gauzy frames of forest and rock, valley floor and surrounding hills. The only sound is the wind—until a raucous jay lands on a branch nearby, then another. My face is cool, damp with snowflakes, but I am warm enough. The only tracks on the road are from a snowplow. Above the horizon, a bright glow strengthens behind and through the clouds, saturating their flat white with drama and motion. I stand still, take a few steps, pivot, stand still again. I am the tiny human figure in a Chinese landscape painting, giving scale to the vast mystery and power of the mountains.

Minutes become a moment. In a swirl of snow, cloud, silence, wind, solitude, and expectation, the year begins.

A couple of hours later, at the end of another road, the scene is very different. In the Bear Lake parking lot, we find ourselves in an impromptu New Year's Day party. It's crowded by winter standards, and most cars have Colorado license plates: good company, neighbors who would rather celebrate the day outside in the mountains than indoors watching football.

We strap on our snowshoes, put lunch in our packs, and head up the trail to Emerald Lake. New snow cushions our steps, more snow falls steadily, and the light is flat, soft, and shadowless. It's quite a contrast from a week ago, when we climbed here on packed snow in the diamond-dust glitter and blue shadows of a sunny day, the warmth of distant fire on our faces, hat brims pulled low to shade our eyes. Now, sheltered by the trees, we feel just a slight breeze, but we see snow plastered on one side of every trunk and, above us, flakes sailing sideways.

Last week we also had the place mostly to ourselves. Now we share it with cheerful dozens of others: snowshoers and skiers, singles and couples, families and friends, babies in baby-packs and sturdy, weathered, walking stick–wielding great-grandparents. We exchange holiday greetings and small talk about the weather and the trail. The crowd thins at pretty little Nymph Lake, frozen and white, and soon the path steepens and grows edgier. We pass giant pink boulders, a frozen waterfall, friendly hikers moving uphill and downhill.

Just before Emerald Lake, our intended destination and lunch spot, the forest opens out and suddenly we are walking directly into the wind. And it's quite a wind! Cold, sharp, loud, straight from miles and miles of mountain snowfields and the ice of glaciers and high lakes. In an instant, tears squirt from my eyes, my nose runs, my skin burns with cold. I wrap my muffler over my face, duck my head into my parka, and turn my back to the wind. John does the same. After more than thirty years of hiking together, we don't need words: we start quickly back down the trail. We aren't here to suffer. Instead we find a sheltered spot where John carves a pair of seats into the snow, then pads them with our extra jackets. Settled in, alone and quiet except when fellow celebrants pass us by, we savor our holiday meal.

Later, driving home, I realize how emblematic this day has turned out to be. Solitude and silence in the morning, a like-minded crowd in the afternoon: Rocky Mountain National Park is both crowded and empty, and the balance between the two shifts by season, day of the week, place, even hour. I admit to preferring the emptier days and places; I love the feeling of being alone in a vast wild space. But I am also beginning to think a little differently about the importance of sharing the park with lots of other visitors. By coming here, and perhaps even more by living our ordinary lives at home, I and all the others who love this place do it damage, however inadvertently. But we also work to protect it, and it is a very good thing that so many of us care enough to do this work.

And it does take work. On the way down from Bear Lake, we drove along a just-widened road, past a giant summer-crowd-control parking lot, through a forest devastated by the mountain pine beetles that have killed millions of trees across the North American West. Lower down, crossing Moraine Park, we glimpsed the edge of the wildfire that burned all through last winter, turning a fire season into a fire year. Now, out of the park and winding down the Big Thompson Canyon heading for the plains, we are in the zone of destruction from the September 2013 floods. This highway reopened only about a month ago, and everywhere I see collapsed hillsides, new pavement on sections of road that evidently washed away, houses and cabins dangling over open space with refrigerators and bed frames hanging loose, piles of debris waiting along the shoulders for next week's first big county trash pickup, raw rock and dirt framing the river.

These are changes that I have watched happen: bigger roads, more people and more cars, dying forests, a longer fire season, heavier rains. Unfolding over days and months, they occur on the timescale and in the rhythms of my own life, though more slowly than today's moment of magic at dawn and festival hours of midday. And all these changes unfold against the backdrop of evolutionary and geological time, rock rising from the planet's interior then cooling into granite, mountain ranges growing and shrinking, continents floating around while glaciers carve and smooth their paths, plants and animals altering their shapes, behavior, and DNA as they respond to their evolving world. This park brings me face-to-face with such different kinds of time: the shortest, the *now, today* of our immediate sensory experience; the longest, *a long time ago, over eons and ages*, the abstract time of knowledge and informed imagination; and, in the middle, the time of our memories and hopes, *this year, during my lifetime*.

Because I came here first as an infant, grew up in nearby Denver, and for the last quarter century have lived just over an hour's drive from the park entrance, I feel at home in these mountains. I've read books as well, carried and consulted field guides, taken a dozen or so outdoor courses here in the park, and I feel reasonably well educated about this place. Yet I have seen very little of everything that is here, everything that happens in these mountains. I have experienced just a few of all their passing days and months. I know just enough to recognize how much there is here that I can still learn about, watch, and explore—and enough to know that the more I learn, the more I see to wonder at, care about and for, appreciate and love. And so I keep paying attention, taking in knowledge, thinking, and working toward wisdom.

One of my best teachers (and, I am honored to say, my friend) is the author of the book in your hands. While by now I know many people who know a lot about Rocky Mountain National Park, Ellen is the most intimate with the land itself and all the complex ways it changes through time, on the scales of *today*, *during my lifetime*, and *over ages and eons*. I have learned a great deal from the engaging book in your hands. I promise that you will, too.

SueEllen Campbell

This is the best of times and the worst of times. Everyday life in the United States is physically easy. Women do not die in their twenties during childbirth or spend most of their waking hours cooking and cleaning. Men do not die in their thirties and forties from physical accidents during work or from exhaustion. On the contrary, we have a great deal of leisure time and we use it to travel and entertain ourselves. As for myself, a woman of modest origins and middle age, I have had the joy of devoting my life to exactly what intrigues me most—the workings of the natural world. Not only can I spend my time following my curiosity where it may lead, I get paid well for doing so. I live close to Rocky Mountain National Park, one of the country's premier natural areas, which has recently celebrated a century of national park status. This is the best of times.

My curiosity has led me into places I never imagined when I started my scientific journeys. I set out to study remote mountain streams in Rocky Mountain National Park, unaware that the top aquatic predator had been fished nearly to extinction and replaced by introduced species. I mapped dozens of logjams in old-growth forest streams, not suspecting the critical role the jams played in retaining nitrogen in an ecosystem being gradually overwhelmed by atmospheric nitrogen inputs from feedlots and tailpipes. I measured peak snowmelt flows, ignorant of the steadily earlier occurrence of these flows each spring as warming climate and windblown dust rushed the snows from the hills. As I learned more about how people are driving environmental change in the national park, I struggled with the weight and responsibilities of the new knowledge. We like to refer to early signs of change as a canary in the coal mine. As one of my colleagues in the climate science community noted, canaries in the coal mine were brought down to die first. This is the worst of times.

In various ways, we each choose a path that reflects the luxuries and indulgences of the best of times, and the responsibilities and urgencies of the worst of times. This book is a collection of personal reflections on our early twenty-first-century times in the context of Rocky Mountain National Park, and an exploration of what makes our times good and bad. I enter the national park as someone who seeks rejuvenation in the natural world. I cannot go too long without spending time in some natural area or something inside me starts to wither. I also perceive the park as a geologist who studies river processes. When I think of the park, I think of a massive block of hard bedrock. The rock has been thrust up from Earth's interior, cooled, and cracked. Gouged by glacial ice, chipped at by freezing and thawing, creased by water, the rock nonetheless remains dominant. Water pools in the depressions and plants are sprinkled lightly over the rock, able to maintain only the shallowest roothold. A strong wind, a heavy rain, or a fire, and the plants are instantly stripped away, their successors left to laboriously regrow over succeeding decades. As a bumper sticker popular with geologists proclaims, "It's all about geology."

My perceptions of the park reflect what I directly experience, what I learn through my research, and what I read. By all of these pathways, I have come to understand that even a national park is marked by the lingering effects of people using this ecosystem over the past two centuries. This is the most difficult lesson to assimilate, for I always want to look at an alpine lake or a ribbon of white water twisting down a rock face and simply appreciate the beauty. Remembering that the lake is slowly acidifying and the white water will dry up earlier in summer than during the past does not diminish the beauty of what I see, but adds an undertone of responsibility for acting to understand and to limit these human-caused changes.

I also think of the park as a much wetter place than it really is, because I work in the wet parts. The scarcity of water in Rocky Mountain National Park defines the rate at which soils form, the types of plants and animals present, and the pace of landscape change. More abundant water, whether over tens of thousands of years during which glaciers advance, or a few days during which streams flood, drives periods of landscape change.

Varying paces of change in the park led me to structure this book around the theme of rhythms. Like any plant or animal in the park, I live my life in annual rhythms based on the weather of each season, but also, in my case, on the academic calendar. I am a professor on the faculty of Colorado State University, with classes to teach during the academic year. Long, physically strenuous days of summer field research alternate with the desk days of winter, when I try to organize and understand the crowded observations of the field season and communicate some of that understanding to my students. The academic year tracks the seasonal year with fall and spring semesters and summer break.

Rhythms in Rocky Mountain National Park over longer time spans are less regular and predictable. Fires spread out from a lightning strike and alter the forest in which I work in ways that will persist for more than a century. Torrential summer rains strip soil and trees from the hillslopes and send streams flooding across the valley bottoms, creating alluvial fans that persist for many centuries. Glaciers advance and retreat over tens of thousands of years. Tectonic energy raises mountains and erosion wears them down over millions of years. These rhythms are punctuated with large changes in a short period of time. Punctuated rhythms create unpredictability. Are we on the cusp of big changes? It's hard to know. Our understanding of climate warming, for example, is a moving target that keeps changing, partly in response to the greenhouse gases we continue to put into the atmosphere and partly because of our limited understanding of exactly how those gases will influence the complicated feedbacks that interact to create climate. People pin their hopes on environmental resilience—the ability of natural systems to absorb change and keep functioning. We also need resilience of people and institutions to help environments remain resilient.

The hundredth anniversary of Rocky Mountain National Park presented an opportunity to contemplate how the natural and human history of the park has shaped present ecosystems and how the varying rhythms of geology, climate, plants and animals, and people have shaped the national park. This book is structured around the seasonal rhythm of a calendar year, but in the chapter for each month I explore some aspect of other longer and shorter rhythms of natural and human history, focusing on a particular place within the park that somehow exemplifies such history.

At least two themes emerge repeatedly in these explorations. The first is the fundamental unevenness of change. Whether considered under the detailed focus of a single year or the grand sweep of millennia, many of the changes in topography and plant and animal communities in the national park take place during a relatively small portion of the time being considered. The rainfall spread over two to three days in September 2013 brought thousands of cubic yards of sediment from steep hillslopes down into valley bottoms. No such large and widespread debris flows had occurred in the park for decades before 2013. Analogously, subsequent geologic processes have barely modified the topography left by glaciers that carved steep-sided troughs into the spine of the continental divide more than 10,000 years ago. Some of the high-elevation forests in which I work have just begun to grow trees as tall as I am more than thirty years after a wildfire. Recognizing the unevenness of changes in natural landscapes and ecosystems through time and across space is critical to understanding how the natural world of Rocky Mountain National Park operates and to managing the national park toward desired conditions. In this book, I explore the causes and consequences of unevenness of change.

The second theme that emerges in exploring the natural communities of the national park is the importance of the unseen. The diverted water that flows far beneath the park in a tunnel, and the invisible dust particles that bring nitrogen to the soil and water

An iconic Rocky Mountain National Park view: Hallett Peak and the continental divide from Sprague Lake.

of the park, create important and persistent changes, of which most park visitors remain unaware. Introduction of exotic species of trout has resulted in changes among the microscopic aquatic insects of subalpine lakes and streams, a historic shift completely unknown to nearly all park visitors, yet a change with potentially important consequences for freshwater ecosystems. With awareness comes insight about the effects of our own choices, and responsibility to choose wisely to best preserve the park that we care about, so I also explore the causes and consequences of unseen changes within the national park.

There is an old curse, "May you live in interesting times." We do. That is our burden, and our opportunity. We can respond effectively to burden and opportunity only if our actions grow from understanding of how natural forces and human actions have shaped the topography and plant and animal communities of the national park. In this book I systematically examine how the natural forces of geology, climate, fire, and interactions among plants and animals have shaped and continue to shape Rocky Mountain National Park. Although the majority of the national park is designated as wilderness, every portion of the park also reflects the influence of human activities, even if this imprint is largely invisible. Consequently, I also systematically explore how historical mining, logging, ranching, tourism, and removal of predators, along with contemporary warming climate, air pollution, fire management, and encroachment of urban areas have shaped and continue to shape the national park. Each of the succeeding chapters focuses on a particular type of natural or human influence on the park and the time and space scales—the rhythms—over which that influence is exerted, but each chapter also reflects the complex interactions among natural and human influences.

January
Wild Basin: Punctuated Rhythms of Geology and Climate

I leave my car at the winter parking area where the road into Wild Basin is closed for the season. As soon as I step out of the car, I am surrounded by a roar. For a moment I think the sound is coming from North St. Vrain Creek, as it would be in summer, then realize that this cannot be: the creek lies buried and muffled beneath thick layers of ice and snow. The roar is wind surging and blasting over the peaks, down the valley, and through the trees, the relentless flow of great masses of air manifested in sound.

I walk a mile to the main trailhead, my snowshoes unneeded on the road along which other hikers have thoroughly compacted the snow. As I hike, I notice more than one tree snapped or uprooted this season, but showing no signs of stress from drought or pine beetles that might have made the tree more susceptible to the wind. The tops of the standing trees are all swaying, from the sides of the road to the silhouettes on the nearest ridge crests, dancing the earnest, high-stakes dance of winter winds. Trunks and branches creak as they move, creating tones so prolonged and varied that it seems the trees are deliberately emitting sounds, like whale song. Conifer needles and bits of bark and lichen litter snow that the wind has wiped clean of small animal tracks. Wind pushes and slams me, creating a sense of the motion of changing seasons, of a planet rushing through space, and of a warming climate redistributing heat across the globe. This is the challenging side of winter, not the restfulness of a landscape asleep under the snow.

The water in an occasional small, open patch along North St. Vrain Creek looks dark against the snow. The patches create viewing windows on a creek that winter has shrouded in mystery. Most of the creatures inhabiting the river wait in suspended animation for the warmth and light that come with spring. Only the water appears alive, frothing and pulsing across the opening before once more vanishing beneath the ice.

This watershed is home ground for me. I have come here repeatedly each summer over many years, trying to understand the hidden goings-on of North St. Vrain Creek. Now I move more slowly and contemplatively along this portion of the creek than I do in summer. Today I have no data to collect, no deadlines to meet. I do not have to watch my footing as I do on this rocky trail in summer. This is the relaxed, steady portion of my annual rhythm, which seems to match the relative quiet of dark water flowing beneath a lid of ice. In summer my pace and the pace of change in the creek pick up considerably. Sometimes I focus on change that occurs at a giddy pace—the minute-to-minute fluctuations in velocity within a pool—but mostly I examine the more sedate patterns that develop over hundreds to thousands of years.

I try to read the landscape, paying careful attention to details and lingering over points I do not understand. Like a complex book, North St. Vrain Creek and its tributaries do not yield their full meaning easily. Insights come after thinking and rethinking over measurements I have made or incidents and patterns I have observed. The process of coming into the country—as a scientist or simply an observant, interested human—requires time and care. I come into this country as a geologist, delving back through the centuries of American and European occupation of the region, beyond the historic and prehistoric Native American tribes, to the time when the valleys of Wild Basin lay beneath hundreds of feet of glacial ice.

What I realize as I come into the country through layers of human and natural history is that change occurs episodically here. At whatever focal length I choose, history resolves into longer periods of relative quiescence interrupted by intervals of rapid change. These are the punctuated rhythms that shape the landscape of the national park.

I am reminded of punctuated rhythms as soon as I don my snowshoes and start along the main trail, which descends a subtle mound next to the parking lot. A little farther upstream, the trail goes over another subtle mound. These mounds are old alluvial fans formed where huge floods on Hunters and Sandbeach Creeks deposited masses of boulders and sand at the junction of each creek with North St. Vrain. The floods occurred hundreds—perhaps even thousands—of years ago, but no flood since then has been able to rework the sediments left by the ancient flood. A few hours of intense erosion of sediment upstream and deposition here on the valley floor, followed by long years during which forest gradually covered the now-stable sediment mounds.

Punctuated Rhythms I: The Glaciers

Despite the snow mantling the steep, forested slopes, there is no obvious sign of past glaciers at the main trailhead of Wild Basin. The trail crosses Hunters Creek and then parallels North St. Vrain Creek upstream. The broad, heavily trampled pedestrian highway of summer is much less visible under snow, but still easy to follow as a broad gap between the trees. After a mile, other trails begin to diverge from the main path. I choose the steep, narrow trail that switchbacks up through the forest along North St. Vrain Creek. At each step I plant the snowshoe firmly to insure a grip that will keep me from sliding backward. I am climbing the trail of a glacier long gone.

Today I can see little but the snow-dusted trees ahead. The heights are an indistinct white cloud, blurred by blowing snow. I know from past experience that the upstream half of the valley of North St. Vrain Creek resembles a hand resting palm upward, with the fingers extending into the air. The fingers are the tributaries—Hunters, Sandbeach, North St. Vrain, Ouzel, and Cony. Each creek begins as a dozen unnamed streamlets of whitewater cascading down steep rock faces and talus slopes into a lake. The lake waters accumulate in a deeper, wider point within each valley, a pause before the creek waters continue their descent into the main North St. Vrain valley.

The uppermost lake along each tributary valley marks the starting point of a Pleistocene valley glacier. A mass of flowing ice carves a valley broader and deeper than that carved by a river. The ice itself cannot carve anything: ice melts under pressure and flows on a layer of liquid water that slips past obstacles. Rocks frozen into the ice and carried along are what makes the glacier a giant adze capable of gouging a valley out of bedrock. Glacial meltwater infiltrates into minute cracks in the underlying rock and then freezes and expands, wedging off pieces of the rock that then freeze into the ice. The landscape is grist for the glacial mill and the rocks become grinding tools as the ice flows onward.

Valley glaciers resemble rivers of ice. Tributary glaciers flow into larger glaciers, increasing the volume of ice flowing downstream. Greater ice volumes carve deeper valleys. Along the portion of North St. Vrain Creek that forms the palm of the hand, glacial ice was 500 feet thick during periods of glacial advance. Glaciers advanced and retreated at least three times during the Pleistocene Epoch of geologic time, from 2 million to 10,000 years ago. Tributary glaciers flowed into the top of the ice mass in the main valley rather than cutting their valleys down to the base of the main glacier. When the ice melted about 15,000 years ago, the tributary valleys were left perched 500 feet above the main valley floor.

Fifteen thousand years later, the tributaries have not been able to catch up and cut down to the level of North St. Vrain Creek. Instead, each creek flows over small steps at logjams and through pools at a gentle gradient to the edge of the main valley, and then falls off the edge, plunging down in long, long waterfalls such as Ouzel Falls and Calypso Cascades.

The punctuated rhythm of Pleistocene glaciations is fast change as the glaciers advance, eroding bedrock and carrying sediment down-valley, creating the broad outlines of the landscape. Then come millennia of relatively little change. Snow, rain, wildfires, rivers, people—none of these have altered the landscape's general configuration very much since the glaciers last retreated.

So what drives the rhythm of the glaciers? The intricate dance of sun and planet. Multiple factors combine to allow enormous volumes of ice to periodically cover large swathes of continent, and then melt back to nothing, but the ultimate driver seems to be the distribution of solar energy reaching Earth's surface. We all count on the rising and setting of the Sun each day, a central metronome of life on Earth. The seasonal changes resulting from the tilt of Earth's axis are equally basic for the rhythms of life at latitudes above the equator. But the relationship between Sun and Earth is not as eternal as we might like to think, or at least Earth is not as consistent in its position with respect to the Sun as we might expect.

First, Earth moves around the Sun as though tethered by an elastic string at varying tension: sometimes Earth's orbit is essentially circular, at other times the orbit is slightly elliptical. The variations in orbital shape, known as eccentricity, are not quite as random as the analogy might make them seem. The orbital shape varies from 0 to 5 percent ellipticity over a cycle that lasts about 100,000 years. Oscillations in the ellipticity are vital to Earth's climate because they alter the distance that the Sun's short wave radiation must travel to reach Earth. At present, Earth's orbit is not very elliptical, so the difference in this distance varies by about 3 percent between the portion of the year when Earth is closest to the Sun and the portion when Earth is farthest from the Sun. This 3 percent difference results in 6 percent more solar energy reaching Earth during January relative to July. During periods of the 100,000-year cycle when the orbit is most elliptical, somewhere between 20 and 30 percent more solar energy reaches Earth during certain portions of the year.

Second, Earth's axis tilts relative to Earth's plane of orbit around the sun. The angle of tilt varies between 21.5 and 24.5 degrees on a cycle that lasts about 41,000 years. Just like ellipticity, variations in tilt influence how solar radiation is distributed between winter and summer. Scientists hypothesize that less tilt promotes the growth of large glaciers by causing warmer winters in which slightly warmer air holds more moisture and drops more snow, which then lingers through the cooler summers.

Finally, Earth wobbles as it spins on its axis, which varies from pointing at the North Star to pointing at the star Vega over a cycle that lasts about 23,000 years. When the axis points toward Vega, seasonal contrasts in temperature are greatest. The formal name for the wobble is precession.

Together, ellipticity, tilt, and precession constitute the Milankovitch Cycles, named for the genius who worked out their mathematics long before computers. Milutin Milankovitch (1879–1958) was a Serbian astronomer and mathematician. Like many who are credited with an amazing new insight, Milankovitch was inspired by the work of others before him. These earlier thinkers suspected that variations in Earth's orbit could explain major climatic shifts and ice ages, but they could not describe the celestial mechanics by which such changes might occur. Having been inadvertently caught on the wrong side of the Austro-Hungarian empire during his honeymoon at the start of World War I, Milankovitch employed four years of "house arrest" in Budapest mathematically working out the relations between solar radiation and temperatures at Earth's surface. Not satisfied with his findings, he developed a mathematical climate model that included reconstructions of past climate and predictions of future climate. Published in 1920, his magnum opus was immediately recognized as a major contribution to understanding climate. Not until the 1960s, however, did methods for determining the age of glacial deposits allow geologists to develop a more precise chronology of glacial advances and retreats and thus rigorously test Milankovitch's hypotheses of past climate. Milankovitch passed the test with flying colors.

Punctuated Rhythms II: Building Mountains and Bringing Them Down

I rest briefly at a rock outcrop on a sharp bend in the trail. The surrounding deep snow confines me to the trail. To step off the trail into the woods in winter is to appreciate the marvelous adaptations of snowshoe hares and the strength of elk and deer, whose tracks through the forest I have been noticing as I climbed.

Below me lies the broad glacial valley of North St. Vrain. Lost in the clouds above are the summits of the Colorado Front Range, a portion of the Southern Rocky Mountains that forms the headwaters of the South Platte River. The Front Range stretches from the Wyoming border 160 miles south and from the continental divide 60 miles east to the edge of the Great Plains. I am nearly at the geographic center of the range. Longs Peak, the highest summit in Rocky Mountain National Park at 14,255 feet, should be in view here, but today I see only low clouds moving in. Three months earlier, one of my colleagues watched an intrepid beaver climbing this same trail, presumably an immigrant from the beaver colony along North St. Vrain Creek at the park's entrance, en route to colonizing a new site higher in the watershed. Today the trail is largely untracked but for the occasional widely spaced imprints of a snowshoe hare's bounding stride.

My breathing gradually slows as I stand still after the steep climb. I am enacting a human dramatization of mountain building, swiftly gaining elevation and then remaining stationary, like the unseen summits around me that rose swiftly and then remained stable. This portion of the Rockies has had its ups and downs over the past 300 million years. Each episode of uplift and mountain building was relatively brief but created the high-elevation peaks and steep hillslopes characteristic of the region. Long stable periods separated the periods of uplift. The mountains were gradually dismantled during the stable times, shedding sediment into adjacent lowlands. The most recent episodes of uplift were about 40 million and then 20 to 5 million years ago. Now the mountains are in a phase of slow dismantling.

Dismantling a mountain range involves breaking rock into unconsolidated sediment and transporting the sediment to lower elevations. Becoming sediment is the fate of all bedrock, but the pathways to that fate vary. Rock expands when overlying material is stripped away, causing minute cracks to form. Water infiltrates into the cracks, freezes, and expands, wedging apart the rock. Swelling plant roots grow into the cracks and give off organic acids that weaken the rock.

Gravity takes over once a portion of the bedrock is physically detached. Rocks fall, shattering in the process. Water and glacial ice flow downslope, carrying along bits of broken rock. Even wind can transport the finest sediment to lower elevations. All of this is slower than the forces that raise mountains. Just as several thousand years of glacial erosion create deep valleys that another several thousand years of river erosion barely begin to modify, the past 5 million years of glacial and river erosion have barely begun to dismantle mountains created during the preceding 15 million years.

The snail's pace of dismantling a mountain range is not solely a reflection of rock that stubbornly resists breakdown and gravity. Geologists speak of glacial buzz saws that rip forcefully into sediment and bedrock, gouging out the valleys that I admire as I rest along the trail. The Colorado River cut the mile-deep Grand Canyon in a few million years, a mere blink of a geologic eye in the course of Earth's history. Part of the persistence of mountains reflects the ability of Earth's crust to flex like a cushion gradually rebounding from the imprint of a sitter's weight.

Think of that satisfying metaphor, "solid as a rock." Ever since I learned geology as an undergraduate, that metaphor has lost its meaning for me. Squeeze a rock hard enough, at pressures experienced below Earth's surface, and the rock flows like tar. Heat the rock hot enough, at temperatures common deep within the planet, and the rock flows like molasses. Anyone who contemplates a contorted layer of rock doubled back on itself and exposed in a mountain cliff can understand that, under sufficient force, rock deforms without shattering. Extend that insight across whole regions of Earth's surface and you can start to conceive of the planet's outer layer, the crust, flexing upward and downward under varying weight just like a chair cushion.

The scientific term for a flexing crust is *isostasy*, a term derived from Greek to describe how the crust "floats" on the underlying mantle at an elevation that depends on the thickness and density of the crust. Think of an iceberg, a famously dangerous object because most of the ice is below the water surface. Mountains are analogous, with a deep root of crust supporting their weight and allowing them to float on the underlying weaker mantle. As erosion removes mass from the mountains, the range rebounds upward. In a sense, glaciers and rivers have to work harder and harder just to stay in place as the crust rebounds in response to their efforts.

I find it relatively easy to understand the big changes that can cause Earth's crust to rise and sink. Mountain building and the formation of continental-scale ice sheets flex the crust downward, and mountain erosion and glacial retreat allow the crust to rebound. These changes do not exactly occur at a dizzying pace by human standards: northern Sweden is still "bounding" upward at nearly four inches a year several thousand years after the glacial ice melted. Nearly four inches a year is pretty impressive, however, for an entire region. What I find more amazing are the subtle flexures. Using sensitive, space-borne and ground instruments, scientists can now detect changes in crustal elevation associated with snow loading and losses of water during periods of drought that last a few years or even a few months.

Many hikers now carry a little global positioning satellite, or GPS, device that helps them determine their location. I always carry one during fieldwork because I can usually quickly record the coordinates of whatever I am studying. (Usually. While working in old-growth rainforests of Costa Rica, I grew accustomed to my GPS asking me the same question every few minutes when I "woke it up" after a period of inactivity. GPS: Have you moved hundreds of miles since your last position? Me, under my breath: No, dammit. This exchange was followed by a frequently futile attempt to find a clearing along the river large enough to pick up a satellite signal.) Scientists studying crustal flexure use higher precision GPS devices attached to solid rock or anchored several feet below the soil to measure displacements in Earth's crust caused by groundwater loss. In 2014, Adrian Borsa, Duncan Agnew, and Daniel Cayan published a scientific paper in which they used eleven years of daily measurements to estimate crustal uplift across the western United States from the Rockies to the Pacific Coast. Among the signals they detected was uplift from groundwater depletion associated with a long drought and continued pumping of regional aquifers. The measured uplift suggested a deficit of 240 gigatons of water, equivalent to a layer of water nearly four inches deep across the entire region. Reading studies such as this one, I imagine Earth's crust flexing over months and years like a sleeper breathing in and out. Perhaps I can think of earthquakes as the sleeper tossing and turning.

Punctuated Rhythms III: A Vertically Zoned World

As I continue upward along North St. Vrain Creek, I leave the upper montane forest and enter the subalpine forest. Scientists classify plant and animal communities within Rocky Mountain National Park into three zones—montane, subalpine, and alpine—based on elevation. These zones reflect a recognition that elevation is destiny for plants and animals in the mountains. Elevation governs climate and the extremes of temperature and moisture that living organisms must withstand. Among these extremes are the natural disturbances—fire, flood, or intense wind—that rearrange the immediate surroundings, destroying some habitat but also creating new habitat. The rhythm of landscape change varies through time in the mountains, but also through space, with different rates of change between the elevation zones.

The montane forest extends from the base of the mountains at about 6,000 feet up to elevations of about 9,000 feet. At time spans of decades to centuries, this is the dynamic zone. Conditions change rapidly every few decades because of wildfires and extreme summer thunderstorms. During the quiet intervals, ponderosa pine, Douglas-fir, Engelmann spruce, and lodgepole pine form a canopy with an open understory of juniper and shrubs. Ground fires that occur every five to thirty years help to keep the understory open but leave the largest trees intact. Then come the game-changers: stand-replacing fires that kill almost all trees but also create opportunities for new seedlings to germinate. Tree rings indicate that forests of the Southern Rockies burn at relatively frequent intervals under natural conditions. Lightning starts a fire during a summer storm and the fire then dances unpredictably across the landscape, burning a stand of trees, skipping across a valley, and burning the opposite hillslope. Before Europeans settled here, stand-replacing fires occurred every forty to one hundred years in the montane forests.

The history of scattered fires left a mosaic of differently aged forest stands, with a patch of forest 30 years old next to an old-growth patch dating from 1650 AD, and then a patch of forest 150 years old. This diversity of tree ages creates diverse habitat for other plants and animals. In summer, I see lovely rose pussytoes growing only under more open forest, but I find the scarlet fruit of baneberry under the dense shade of old-growth forest. Old-growth montane forest is rare, however. These forests were too accessible to those wielding axes during the nineteenth century, and only small, isolated old-growth forests persist. Much of the montane forest within the national park is only 100 to 140 years old.

Besides changing the montane forest, wildfires make hillslopes more vulnerable to erosion during summer thunderstorms. An intense fire kills standing trees and vaporizes the undergrowth, leaving hillslope sediment exposed and easy for water to erode. The first heavy rainfalls following a fire are likely to strip the slopes down to bedrock. The thick layer of fallen pine needles and decayed plant material is gone, so the rainfall does not infiltrate and move gradually downslope within the soil. Instead, water sluices down the barren slopes, carrying along sediment, creating a flash flood or a sediment-laden debris flow. Measurements of sediment coming off hillslopes over a period of decades show that the great majority of sediment moves during a tiny fraction of the time, primarily after wildfires.

Rainfall can also trigger large floods in the absence of fires, but mostly at elevations lower than those in the national park. Spring snowmelt causes the normal yearly flood, which is relatively well behaved because predictable. The snowpack can be measured throughout the winter, providing an indication of the total water available for melting, and the flooding usually occurs relatively gradually. Rainfall flash floods triggered by intense summer and autumn storms are much less predictable. The waters of a rainfall flood can rise with terrifying suddenness over an hour or two, creating a much larger flood peak than snowmelt floods.

The thunderstorms that create flash floods in the Front Range result primarily from moist air masses moving inland from the Gulf of Mexico. These air masses have a long journey over the plains before reaching the mountains. Every time the air rises in passing over a topographic blip, such as the hills at the base of the Rockies, the air cools and some of the moisture that it carries condenses and falls as rain. By the time the air reaches the summits of the Rockies within the national park, much of the moisture has already been wrung out. This is not to say that rain cannot fall hard in the park: anyone who has been caught in a summer downpour knows otherwise. But these downpours do not last very long at the higher elevations. It is the middle elevations of the Rockies—approximately 8,000 feet and lower in the Front Range—that can receive the truly epic rainfalls. During the July 1976 storm that caused massive flooding in Big Thompson Canyon, twelve inches of rain fell in two days in some locations below the national park. The September 2013 storm brought six to nine inches of rain to Estes Park in four days, but up to fifteen inches fell on Boulder—2,100 feet lower—during the same period. Like the long-lasting mounds along the North St. Vrain trail built by floods, the 1976 flood created bars and alluvial fans along the

Big Thompson River that no subsequent snowmelt flood was able to move.

The big events—glaciers, fires, floods—create a landscape template that persists until the next big event. I think of the old cliché about army life consisting of long periods of boredom interspersed with moments of sheer terror. Creating and shaping a landscape consists of long periods of stability interspersed with moments when all hell breaks loose. Like a fractal pattern that presents the same level of complexity as I look more and more closely, the pace of landscape change is episodic at whatever timescale I consider, from hundreds of millions of years, to millennia, centuries, decades, or even a single year.

As I continue up the trail into the subalpine zone, I enter a more sedate world in terms of landscape change occurring over tens to hundreds of years. Lodgepole pine, Engelmann spruce, subalpine fir, and limber pine dominate the subalpine forest. Change does occur here: much of the forest is younger than 200 years as a result of past wildfires, blowdowns by intense winds, or timber harvest that occurred before the national park was designated in 1915. But in less accessible portions of the park—Forest Canyon along the Big Thompson River, the upper portions of the Glacier Creek watershed, and the upper portions of Wild Basin—many of the trees are older than 200 years. This is the forest primeval, the forest where giants too large in girth to be completely hugged form a canopy that shuts out much of the sunlight. In this forest, fallen trees decay so slowly that the trunks can persist for hundreds of years, forming a dense tangle difficult to penetrate on foot away from the trail. This is also the forest rich in silences, where a human presence can trigger a five-minute tirade from a squirrel perched on a spruce branch overhead, the animal's entire body shaking with the vigor of its displeasure.

It takes a lot to disturb this forest, which is one reason that trees can persist into old age. Fires are less frequent here than at lower elevations: stand-killing fires occur on average only once every

300 to 400 years. Rainfall is less intense and less likely to trigger the debris flows that strip hillslopes of trees and soil. Winds can be intense, with gusts reaching ninety miles per hour. Microbursts can rip up entire trees or shear the trunk into two pieces, but such violence seldom affects areas of more than a few acres at a time.

Between disturbances, the subalpine forest ages in predictable patterns. Lodgepole pines colonize a site first, with hundreds of seedlings germinating and growing into "dog-hair" stands of dense, spindly trees. After a century, some of these trees die off. The forest thins itself, growing into larger, more widely spaced trees. Spruce and fir germinate in the shade created by the lodgepole pines. As the spruce and fir grow to maturity, they replace the lodgepoles as the dominant trees. By 200 years, the forest achieves old-growth status, with an abundance of large, old trees, as well as plenty of snags (standing dead trees), logs on the forest floor, and a multi-layered canopy.

The Pleistocene glaciers have been the primary agents of landscape change within the subalpine zone during the past 2 million years. Much of the montane zone was too dry to support glaciers: even the largest valley glaciers barely extended down below 9,000 feet. Similarly, much of the alpine tundra above the subalpine forest was too dry and windy to allow snow to collect and form glacial ice. The subalpine zone was the sweet spot for valley glaciers and here the big ice left its enduring mark on the landscape.

As I continue upward within the subalpine forest, the wind grows even stronger and the creaking and cracking of the trees sounds ominous. I turn back well below timberline. Lost in snow and clouds above lies the alpine tundra, the landscape above 11,350 feet, where trees cannot survive. The tundra is the place where summer lightning can strike with such violence that it leaves a trench in the ground and winter storms can blast subzero air across the terrain with gale force. Despite the short-term drama of weather fluctuations in the tundra, this part of the park is a remarkably stable landscape. Much of the tundra is a gently rolling

Gently rolling tundra uplands above Bear Lake in Rocky Mountain National Park during summer.

plateau on which bedrock weathers slowly and sediment remains in place. Fires seldom burn the tundra. The vertical rock walls that challenge gravity are uncommon. The area is too high and dry to have the prolonged heavy rainfalls that cause flash floods. This landscape covered by alpine plants simply endures.

Punctuated Rhythms IV: Hot Spots and Hot Moments

I follow the trail down to one of my study sites along North St. Vrain Creek, working nearly as hard to keep from sliding down steep portions of the trail in my snowshoes as I did to keep from sliding backward while climbing. I started studying the creek several years ago when I mapped all of the downed dead wood along the mainstem and the primary tributaries. The mapping extended through a long, physically strenuous summer during which I watched a pair of sturdy hiking boots gradually detach along the seams until they looked more like oddly designed sandals. A sense of urgency underlay the mapping, because I knew that a period of change was coming. The mountain pine beetle (*Dendroctonus ponderosae*), a native beetle that kills several species of conifers, was spreading rapidly from Colorado's western slope forests eastward toward Rocky Mountain National Park. Broad tracts of dead and dying trees spread across watersheds in which I had worked on the western slope. I wanted to document the amount of wood along creeks in the national park before the trees started dying and falling over.

My original intent of establishing baseline data that I could use to assess change broadened rapidly. The maps that resulted from that summer's work (long, rolled pieces of paper that one of my colleagues calls the Dead Wood Scrolls) revealed hot spots rich in logjams along each creek. Biochemists use the phrases *hot spots* and *hot moments* to describe the relatively small places and short time intervals in which a disproportionate amount of chemical change occurs. An individual logjam creates a hot spot along a stream. Water forced into the streambed upstream from a logjam flows a short distance through the shallow subsurface beneath the bed before welling up into the channel again. During this short journey the water undergoes microbial magic: microbes living in the sediment consume nitrogen for their own needs, reducing the concentrations of nitrogen in the water welling back up into the creek.

Relatively short stream segments of wide valley bottom and old-growth forest are also hot spots with larger and more closely spaced logjams. The jams block flow in the creeks, forcing the snowmelt floods out across the valley bottom and creating a maze of smaller channels that branch and rejoin. These smaller channels also collect fallen wood in logjams. The backwater pool above each logjam stores pine needles, twigs, and leaves on which microbes and aquatic insects can feast, growing plentiful enough to feed the trout, ouzels, and other large animals of the river ecosystem.

Between these hot spots rich in logjams are the steep, narrow portions of the creek down which stream flow carries twigs and leaves far too fast for microbes and insects to do anything but watch hungrily as the food zips by.

The annual snowmelt flood of early summer is a prolonged hot moment, the portion of the year when streams carry the greatest amounts of sediment, organic matter, and dissolved nutrients. This is when stream insects, fish, and riverside insects and birds speed through breeding, birth, and growth to maturity. The faster pace of change along the creeks—with stream flow and channel form changing daily—as well as the easier access of summer, usher in my own prolonged hot moment of summer field research and a succession of long days hiking up to remote portions of each creek to make measurements.

Now I stand beside the creek, straining to hear the muffled sounds of water flowing beneath a lid of snow and ice at a logjam amidst the ruckus of the wind. This is a very cold hot spot today, but I know that things will soon start to happen as the warmth of spring sends melting snow flowing down the slopes and along the channels, providing the liquid water that initiates a season of new growth. I turn in a slow circle, scanning the surrounding forest. Trees attacked by beetles are starting to fall over, creating more logjams but also making it difficult to even reach the creek in some places. I feel fortunate to be able to watch this portion of forest and creek year after year, observing new logjams form, grow, and then break up. As I come back to the same places each year, I experience my own hot moments of insight. One summer day, midway through a long, grueling hike down Sandbeach Creek, the presence of a huge boulder bar covered in mature forest triggered the revelation that a very large, prehistoric flood had come down the creek. Where I stand now, the sight of clear water bubbling up well back from the creek during a dry autumn provided compelling evidence of the subsurface flow facilitated by logjams.

Today the air is too chill for me to linger long beside the creek.

I feel like an alien here in winter, unable to relax enough to remain still for long, let alone take a nap or lose myself in contemplation as I can in summer. I am intensely aware that I could not long survive in these temperatures. Conscious of my vulnerability, I have even more admiration for the animals that live here year-round. I scan the mysterious topography of winter—depths hidden by drifts, obstacles of snow-buried logs and boulders, and odd slopes and ledges of ice on the creek—and turn back to follow the trail down to Ouzel Falls. The falls are buried, only snow-grizzled icicles lacing together the snow mounds. Snow crystals blast into space from the lip of the falls like wind-blown spray in summer, sparkling in the last rays of sunlight as storm clouds advance down the valley.

Soon, the wind calms and the air is thick with falling snow that muffles sounds. I move through a white landscape quiet but for the occasional chirp of a chickadee or a nuthatch. Reddish brown streaks of tree bark contrast with the falling snow. Small tufts of snow build on the ends of the fir branches before cascading softly to the ground, where they leave an indentation that new snow quickly fills. I feel sheltered from winds and falling snow, as though the forest had gathered in like a warm blanket about my shoulders. A moose rises to its feet from its resting area beneath a large spruce. Neither of us breaks the silence of the winter forest and I continue on my way.

A slick of clear ice covers the trail where groundwater seeps from the hillside. Like the creek, the ice is a reminder that liquid water continues to flow within this landscape despite the chilling air temperatures. I think about the warmth that waits for me indoors, and about how ecosystems and landscape change in the park result from hot spots and hot moments—the places where the logjams form and the episodes when the fires burn, the slopes fail, the glaciers advance, or the mountains are forced up. These are punctuated rhythms that I find fascinating. I smile, remembering Ira Gershwin's line, "Fascinating rhythm, you've got me on the go!"

The Colorado is the iconic river of the American Southwest, a river of desert canyons and red-rock plateaus, and of muddy water flowing thick with silt and clay. But at its origins, the Colorado is a river of mountains and glacial valleys, flowing clear and cold through cobble-bedded pools and riffles. The origins of the Colorado River are a matter of contention and of booster pride. One branch of the river, the Green, comes down from Wyoming's Wind River Range. Another branch comes down from the western side of Rocky Mountain National Park. Early Colorado politicians, eager to associate the state with the river, made sure this branch was named the Colorado, even though the Wyoming headwaters drain a larger area.

People manipulated the flow and landscapes of the upper Colorado River for decades before Rocky Mountain National Park was established in 1915. Like Wild Basin, the natural landscape of the upper Colorado reflects the geologic rhythms of mountain building and glaciations and the climatic rhythms of snowmelt floods and summer rains. People have altered these rhythms by redistributing water and sediment across the landscape, with consequences that we are still trying to understand.

The Geologic Underpinnings

Skiing into the upper Colorado valley in February from Trail Ridge Road, I cannot easily perceive the glacial sculpting of the valley. From the broad segment of the continental divide at La Poudre Pass, one valley glacier flowed north and east down the Cache la Poudre valley. Another flowed south and west down the upper Colorado valley. Glaciers on the western side of the divide, in the Colorado drainage, were larger than those on the eastern side, just as the western side today is slightly wetter. The spine of the Never

Summer Mountains forms the western boundary of the upper Colorado valley, and someone with a sense of humor, or a sense of the fitting, named some of the highest peaks Mount Stratus, Mount Nimbus, Mount Cumulus, and Thunder Mountain. Lake of the Clouds feeds one of the tributaries to the Colorado.

As I continue upstream, the valley expands into broad meadows and wetlands that now form an undulating surface beneath the snow. Forests of dark green spruce and pines cover the steep side slopes of the valley. Today the upper valley walls disappear into low clouds. The base of each wall eases down into treeless alluvial fans and then steps down once more to the channel, where a thin stream of water still flows openly between thick snow banks. The alluvial fans that rumple the edges of the valley floor reflect a long history of sediment shed from the adjacent valley walls, commonly quite abruptly, which accumulated along the margins of the valley. The bedrock underlying these walls is among the most unstable in the park because of its history of being baked and steamed as the mountains were built. On this detail of geology turn the history and contemporary management dilemmas of the upper Colorado River. But first, the geologic story.

The creation of a mountain range is a violent, messy process. Rocks are compressed, sheared, and forced upward, shattering along faults, melting and flowing under the intense heat and pressure. Water and gases can be squeezed from the molten rock and shoot off toward the surface following cracks in the rock, carrying along dissolved chemicals. When the temperature and pressure decrease as the fluids rise toward the surface, minerals crystallize along the sides of the bedrock cracks. These minerals form the veins of precious metals that miners work so hard to extract. The minerals also form deposits that are not economically valuable, but that do weaken the bedrock and make the rock more susceptible to weathering and erosion.

To the west of my route, between Mount Nimbus and Mount Cumulus, stands Red Mountain, named for the minerals that streak its flanks with broad swaths of red, orange, and purple. Farther upstream lies the portion of the Colorado River valley known as the Little Yellowstone for its resemblance to the vivid hues of the volcanic rocks along the Grand Canyon of the Yellowstone River in Wyoming.

The deposition of minerals that left the bedrock along the upper Colorado River stained with sunset hues created small gold deposits. All around the national park—in parts of the Poudre River drainage to the north, in Boulder Creek to the southeast, and especially in Clear Creek farther south—fabulous wealth was wrested from the ground in lode and placer mines. The park was spared the accompanying devastation of forests and streams largely because it lay outside of the gold-rich zones. A little of the golden ore did rise to the surface within the park, however, and the gold gave rise to Lulu City.

When nineteenth-century miners found gold along this portion of the upper Colorado in 1875, cabins quickly went up. The population of Lulu City grew to as many as 500 as would-be millionaires worked the valley-bottom sediment with shovels and sluices, separating the heavier placer gold from the chunks of quartz and other minerals. Not enough gold was present to support the miners, however, and they abandoned the site by 1885. Today the rotting foundations of a log cabin to one side of the trail are the most obvious remnant of what is still designated on the park map as Lulu City, to the confusion of at least one pair of British tourists who hiked in on a summer morning expecting to be able to breakfast in a restaurant.

The more lasting effect of the mineral deposition is the tendency of the bedrock along the upper Colorado River to weather and erode more rapidly than other portions of the national park, sending debris flows—slurries of rock, mud, and water—tumbling down the slopes to the valley bottom. Hillslopes collapse more frequently in this portion of the valley than anywhere else in the park. This fact escaped the nineteenth-century water engineers who

The Upper Colorado River valley in 2008.

were the next people to seek wealth from the resources of the upper Colorado after the miners.

Water Flows toward Money

I develop a soothing rhythm of kick-and-glide as I continue upstream across the alluvial fans. Down to my left, I glimpse a moose among the small patches of willows remaining beside the creek. The lack of willows is not as noticeable in summer when the whole valley bottom seems luminous with a more vibrant shade of green than the adjacent valley walls. Now the absence of willows is striking. Snow buries the grasses, leaving the isolated, heavily browsed, stubby little willows looking particularly pathetic.

If the moose sees me, it gives no sign. Thomas Andrews traces the progress of moose in the Upper Colorado region in *Coyote Valley*, his comprehensive history of this portion of the national park. In 1978, the Colorado Department of Wildlife began to transplant moose to the western slopes of the Never Summer Range just beyond the national park. By 1980 the moose had reached the western side of the park and within little more than a decade the growing moose population, along with elk reintroduced to the national park, appeared to be over-browsing willow thickets along the Upper Colorado. This dramatically reduced the food supply for beavers in the valley. Beavers had survived early nineteenth-century fur trapping and later nineteenth-century agricultural settlement and draining of wet meadows for hay cultivation. A 1939 census counted approximately 600 beavers in this portion of the Upper Colorado. Today, however, I do not expect to see any signs of recent beaver activity.

As I pause to watch the moose, I wonder how much the low level of flow that I see in the river reflects the presence of the Grand Ditch far up on the opposite side of the valley. Grand Ditch probably has little influence on the Colorado's flow at this time of the year, but once snowmelt starts in spring, the ditch will intercept much of the stream flow along tributaries to the upper Colorado. The story of how a ditch came into existence in this remote upper valley is intertwined with the history of gold mining.

The 1859 discovery of gold near Denver initiated a series of rushes for gold, silver, and other precious metals that continued into the early twentieth century. Many of those who rushed into Colorado never got rich from minerals, but there was money to be made in selling supplies to the miners and there was land for agriculture. The new immigrants founded a string of towns along the eastern base of the Front Range, connected to the mining centers and the rest of the world via the rapidly expanding railroad network and utterly dependent on water diverted from rivers to support their crops.

The South Platte and its mountain tributaries head near the continental divide, swelling each May and June with snowmelt runoff and then shrinking back to a much smaller flow by late summer. Within a decade of the first gold strike, most of the water in these rivers was legally claimed and diverted into crop fields. Continued population growth and economic expansion required additional water sources. People quickly looked to the wetter, western slope of the continental divide, with its abundant Colorado River flowing downstream and out of the state, barely tapped by the sparse human population of the western slope. A common joke in Colorado is that water flows toward money rather than following the dictates of gravity.

Water can flow toward money because of the prior appropriation doctrine, which governs water use in Colorado and across the western United States. In many wet regions of the world, water use is governed by the riparian doctrine, which equates proximity to a watercourse with right to use the water. Miners rushing to California's gold fields after the 1849 discovery at Sutter's Mill came up with a new way to allocate water because of their pressing need for abundant flowing water. Many of these miners worked placer deposits in which precious metals are mixed with large quantities of nonprecious sand, cobbles, and boulders in stream valleys. Denser gold preferentially separates from the other sediment when everything is agitated in water. This is the simple principle that governs use of a gold pan, with its sides ridged to trap the gold particles, or a wooden flume with a metal bottom, known as a rocker box. Water is absolutely necessary to separate the gold. If someone began to work a placer deposit upstream from an existing mining claim, the upstream users might divert all of the stream flow, effectively rendering the downstream claim worthless. Prior appropriation was designed to avert this calamity by guaranteeing water rights to claimants based on when they filed for the water rights. Consequently, prior appropriation is usually summarized as "first in time, first in right." A miner who found a rich placer deposit away from a contemporary stream would have been out of luck, except that prior appropriation quickly evolved to allow water to be diverted from the stream, and to be sold or transferred like any other form of property.

Farmers settling the semiarid grasslands at the eastern base of the Rocky Mountains quickly adapted the legal framework of prior appropriation, which allowed someone investing hard work and money into farm fields to be guaranteed the ability to divert stream flow for irrigation, regardless of who settled upstream. As numerous agricultural communities grew north and south of Denver, however, all of the existing stream flows on the South Platte River and its mountain tributaries were quickly appropriated, limiting future growth. That was when people began to eye the headwaters of the Colorado River and other water sources on the far side of the mountains.

The Grand Ditch was the first of many diversions of water across the continental divide and an impressive engineering feat when the first phase of construction was completed in 1892. Using tools as simple as picks, shovels, and dynamite, people took water flowing to the Pacific Ocean and directed it instead toward the Atlantic. Whatever else the Grand Ditch may be, it is a monument to the attitude that any landscape, ecosystem, or natural process can be rearranged to suit human desires.

Begun before the designation of Rocky Mountain National Park, the Grand Ditch was allowed to remain within park boundaries following a series of complicated negotiations and boundary adjustments to the park that were not completed until 1930. Today the ditch creates a distorted reflection of the upper Colorado River. Water in the ditch flows parallel to water in the river but perched 800 feet higher on a steep valley wall, flowing north while the river flows south. The ditch diverts water across La Poudre Pass and down the Poudre River for distribution among the cities and farm fields of the eastern slope of the Rockies.

The presence of Grand Ditch within the national park is more than just a historic anachronism. The ditch creates hazards and management challenges for the park service. The ditch catches small debris flows and rockfall from the steep slopes above. If the ditch is not carefully maintained, this sediment can fill it, forcing water over the sides during snowmelt runoff. Because the ditch is unlined, flow can also seep into its bed and the underlying hillslope. Both seepage and overtopping can trigger large debris flows that move quickly down the steep valley walls and into the Colorado River. In *Coyote Valley*, Thomas Andrews writes of at least three episodes of debris flows and breaches along the ditch during the 1960s and 1970s, which prompted complaints from park visitors and "the ire of the Park Service."

Then came May 2003, when an enormous debris flow started at the ditch and surged down the steep channel of Lulu Creek, a tributary to the Colorado River on the western side of the valley. The debris flow created a large fan at the confluence of Lulu Creek and the Colorado River, then continued down the Colorado River valley to the broad meadow and wetland around Lulu City. Here the debris flow lost momentum and deposited an estimated 48,000 cubic yards of sediment (enough to cover a football field with sediment nearly three feet thick) on the valley floor, burying the channel and the wetlands under more than three feet of sediment.

The National Park Service, understandably, was not happy with the private company that operates Grand Ditch. The US Department of Justice, representing the park service, sued the company. The lawsuit was eventually settled out of court for several million dollars, but the park service was left with some challenging questions. Given the tendency of the hillslopes along the upper Colorado River to weather and erode more rapidly than bedrock in other areas of the park, did the presence of Grand Ditch really increase the size or frequency of debris flows? What should be done following the 2003 debris flow to restore the river and the wetlands?

Altered Rhythms?

On this February day the Lulu City wetland appears serene and undisturbed, with nothing to distinguish it particularly from the surrounding snow-covered landscape. Summer will again reveal that even though several years have passed, less vegetation grows on the 2003 debris flow sediment. The sediment resembles a pale gray scab across the valley bottom—not a bleeding wound of completely bare and eroding sediment, but not a fully healed swath of lush meadow, either.

My friend and fellow geologist Sara Rathburn tackled the question of whether Grand Ditch had increased debris flows coming into the upper Colorado River valley. First she had to characterize debris flow history in the absence of the ditch. When a geologist, ecologist, or other natural scientist tries to determine whether historical or contemporary human activities have altered an ecosystem, the scientist commonly tries to characterize the natural range of variability of the system. Natural range of variability describes the fluctuations through time and space that occur independently of human actions. The Upper Colorado River, for example, experiences increases in flow during each year's snowmelt. Particularly large snowmelt flows can deepen pools, preferentially remove finer sediment from the streambed, erode the channel banks, or rearrange wood in the channel. Periodically, a debris flow introduces a large amount of wood and sediment into the channel, partially filling the pools, coarsening the streambed, or changing the width of the channel. Different aspects of channel form change repeatedly through time, and the fluctuations define some range of variability between, for example, maximum and minimum channel width. One way to infer whether human actions such as flow diversion or timber harvest have altered a stream is to demonstrate whether fluctuations in channel characteristics following the human activity exceed fluctuations associated with the natural range of variability.

This sounds relatively straightforward, but can be as

View down Lulu Creek a few years after the 2003 debris flow. The extent of the debris flow is marked by the freshly deposited sediment, which appears pale gray.

complicated as rocket science. Being able to quantify natural range of variability depends on developing records of channel change prior to human alteration. Sometimes this can be accomplished by finding a channel with otherwise similar characteristics that has not been subject to human influences. The unaltered channel is known as a reference site. In many regions of the world today, however, finding a reference site is extraordinarily difficult or impossible because of the ubiquity of human alterations. Sometimes natural range of variability can be inferred from sedimentary or botanical records of channel form prior to the human alteration. Sara used a combination of these approaches to examine the potential influence of the Grand Ditch on the Upper Colorado River.

Nineteenth-century gold miners and ditch diggers were not recording the size and frequency of debris flows, but such records do exist in the sediments filling the valley of the Colorado River and in the rings of trees growing along the valley walls. Working with graduate students Zan Rubin and Kyle Grimsley, Sara examined the valley-bottom sediments through radar imaging and pits dug into the valley floor and used tree rings to map the ages of trees growing on debris-flow deposits along both sides of the valley.

Buried beneath the valley surface are sediments recording environments past: sand and silt ponded behind beaver dams in a place where active beaver colonies are no longer present; peat deposited in wet marshes; and boulders dropped by debris flows. Sara and Zan imaged this buried sediment using ground-penetrating radar or GPR. GPR transmits a high-frequency electromagnetic pulse into the ground. The pulse is partially reflected back to the surface where there are changes in the electrical properties of the subsurface materials, such as contacts between deposits of different grain size, mineral or water content, or boundaries between sediment and bedrock. Electromagnetic pulses of different frequency provide different levels of information. Lower frequency signals penetrate deeper into the ground but with lower resolution. A 50 megahertz antenna, for example, can penetrate to 26 feet with just over 9 inches of vertical resolution, whereas a 200 megahertz antenna penetrates less than 7 feet but with 2.5 inches of resolution. So, back and forth Sara and Zan went, surveying lines across the valley bottom and down the center of the valley with different antennae, generating images with densely spaced squiggly black lines resembling the "no signal" patterns on a television with bad reception.

The art to the science is detecting patterns within the squiggly black lines and inferring the causes of those patterns. The ability to actually see what you are imaging, and calibrate the type of GPR signal that a particular material creates, is immensely helpful. In this respect, Sara and Zan had access to information normally unobtainable in the minimal disturbance zone of a national park. Given the need to understand potential long-term effects of the Grand Ditch, the National Park Service obligingly helicoptered in a backhoe and dug trenches nearly 12 feet deep into the valley bottom sediment so that Sara and Zan could calibrate the GPR images against known sediments.

Extrapolating from these small "known sites" to the rest of the valley sediment imaged with GPR, and using bits of charcoal and wood dispersed within the sediment to obtain radiocarbon ages, Sara and Zan found that Grand Ditch has increased debris flows reaching the valley bottom. During a period of about 4,000 years before the construction of the ditch, sediment accumulated in the upper Colorado River valley at rates of less than an inch to about 8 inches per century. After the ditch, this rate increased to nearly 16 inches per century.

The pre-ditch accumulation of sediment marks the punctuated rhythms inherent in natural processes, which define the natural range of variability. More sediment layered the valley bottom during centuries of cooler, drier climate. By quantifying the upper and lower values of sediment accumulation in the Upper Colorado valley through time prior to the Grand Ditch, Sara and Zan demonstrated that the rate of sediment accumulation has increased above these values since construction of the ditch, exceeding the natural range of variability for the valley.

Sara and Zan also used reference sites to assess how well the Upper Colorado River was recovering from the excess sediment introduced by the 2003 debris flow. They compared rates of sediment movement, sizes of sediment on the channel bed, and channel form between the Upper Colorado and streams unaffected by Grand Ditch. Between 2003 and 2009, channel form and process on the Upper Colorado River gradually recovered to levels comparable to those of reference sites, demonstrating the sometimes remarkable resiliency of rivers.

Pursuing another line of evidence to understand the potential effects of Grand Ditch, Sara and graduate student Kyle Grimsley measured the location and volume of alluvial fans that debris flows deposited along the margins of the Colorado River valley, determined the age of trees growing on these fans, and used tree cores to determine the dates at which debris flows had scarred trees that survived the battering by boulders. They found that six of the ten alluvial fans are on the western side of the river valley, the side with the Grand Ditch. Tree ages covering nearly a century (1923–2003) indicate that several of these fans have been built by multiple debris flows. Debris flows have not occurred more frequently on the western side, but three of the four largest debris flows within the past century have come from the western side, suggesting that Grand Ditch has increased the number of debris flows large enough to spread across the valley bottom and reach the channel of the Upper Colorado River.

The converging lines of evidence that Grand Ditch has increased debris flows to the valley bottom left the tougher question of what to do about the 2003 debris flow sediments. One alternative is to do nothing, allowing the river to redistribute the sediments and allowing the wetland plants to grow back as they are able. Another option is to helicopter in heavy equipment and scrape off all the debris-flow sediments to reveal the buried wetland beneath.

A Managed Wilderness

On sunlit winter days, the snow is a source of light, reflecting sunshine from the facets of an infinite number of snow crystals to create a landscape of vibrant, almost blinding shades of blue and white. On overcast winter days like today, the snow seems to absorb the light, creating a landscape of somber shades of gray, white, and dark green.

The cheerful dee-dee-dee of a chickadee's call from the nearby forest is like audible sunlight and reminds me of the other, unseen wildlife of the surrounding forest and meadow. When I enter a national park, I expect to find a place that appears natural, where plants and animals live within their own communities and on their own terms dictated by geology, climate, wildfires, and other plants and animals, but not humans. The scab of the 2003 debris flow sediment and the boulder-filled trench of Lulu Creek do not meet these expectations, but neither would the sound and sight of helicopters and backhoes.

Regardless of the specific scenario that the park service chooses for the upper Colorado River, the site exemplifies the dilemmas inherent in resource management within Rocky Mountain National Park. Ninety-five percent of the national park is designated as wilderness that is supposed to receive minimal management and human intervention. But Rocky Mountain is neither a pristine wilderness nor a completely natural environment. Top predators such as wolves and grizzly bears have been missing for nearly a century. The park is closely surrounded by more intensively managed lands, from the cities of Estes Park and Grand Lake, to the adjacent national forest lands where beetle-killed trees are cut and removed. And the park is inevitably connected to the greater landscape. Nitrates blow in on the upslope winds on the eastern side of the park and this acidifies high-elevation soils and streams. Dust blows in from the southwestern United States and from points as far beyond as China, and the dark dust settling on the snowfields causes the snowpack to melt more rapidly. Above all else, the park is subject to a steadily warming climate and all the surprises that may bring. Under these conditions, the core backcountry areas of the park are wilderness in some sense, but are nonetheless far from untouched by human actions.

Setting land aside as a national park and further protecting it with wilderness designation is only the start. Because of continuing human influences, park personnel have to manage the wilderness. Difficult as it can be to achieve protected status for a region, managing the protected lands is more difficult. Ongoing management involves subtle, nuanced interpretations of what is best for the ecosystem. Our collective interpretation of what is best changes through time as our understanding of ecosystem history and processes changes.

I grow chilled as I stand listening to the chickadee and pondering these dilemmas. Yet even on this chill, cloudy day, I sense the gathering energy of the coming spring. The hours of daylight are noticeably increasing, and when the sun appears it crosses the sky farther to the north.

Like the annual return of spring and the season of reproduction and growth, this valley bottom can recover from disturbances such as debris flows. The Colorado River now soaks into the sediments from the 2003 debris flow, leaving only a shallow channel at the surface, but the river will eventually rework the sediment and re-create a more defined channel. The wetland plants will once again cover the bars that are now bare sand and gravel. Beavers may even return if controlled populations of moose and elk allow seedling willows and aspen to grow large and numerous enough to provide food for a beaver colony. River ecosystems are remarkably resilient to episodic pulses of extra water and sediment. But changing the rhythm of these pulses—making them stronger and more frequent—can force the ecosystem across a tipping point into a persistent new configuration. The beaver meadows and floodplain wetlands can be buried too deeply and frequently to recover and the valley bottom can change to a drier grassland environment.

Contemporary management of park lands strives to understand the natural range of variability for each ecosystem within the park. This is where the specialized skills of geologists and ecologists become important as these scientists read the landscape, assembling and interpreting evidence of changes through time. Ideally, scientific knowledge helps park managers to minimize human actions that could sufficiently alter the natural rhythms to drive the ecosystem beyond natural variability.

I ski down to the river's edge and lean over the tall banks of compacted snow. Removing my mitten, I lower my bare hand briefly into the cold water. My fingers immediately numb and then burn as I pull my hand back. I find it difficult to believe that anything can survive in this frigid water, but somewhere under the brown and gray cobbles of the streambed, larval caddisflies and mayflies wait for the warmth and sunlight of spring. Trout hold a steady position in areas of slow current, waiting for their metabolism to kick into higher gear as the insects emerge and the stream begins to flow more strongly. For the river and its inhabitants, this tail end of winter is a time of slow rhythms until the melting snow hurries everything along. If the park service can work with the managers of Grand Ditch to prevent future failures of the ditch, the melting snows will eventually hurry the 2003 sediment far enough along to allow the Upper Colorado River valley to recover.

The view west from Moraine Park is one of the most iconic in Rocky Mountain National Park. Entering the national park from the eastern side, as most visitors do, the broad, treeless valleys of Hollowell Park, Moraine Park, Beaver Meadows, and Horseshoe Park provide the most sweeping views of the peaks of the continental divide. Across the Rocky Mountain West, nineteenth-century fur trappers called these grassy valleys surrounded by mountains either parks or holes, as in Jackson Hole, Wyoming. When I visit Moraine Park, I look west across a foreground shaped by Pleistocene glaciers advancing and then retreating; beavers building dams, creating wet meadows, and then leaving; and people building homes and recreational facilities, then removing these signs of human engineering. The view west from Moraine Park encapsulates the natural and human history of the national park.

I am here on the cusp of spring to send radar waves into the ground. This sounds vaguely menacing, but my students and I are not irradiating earthworms: we are trying to create images of what lies below the ground surface, just as Sara and Zan did along the Upper Colorado River. Today is a test run for the prolonged work we will conduct during the summer. As we cross the broad, grassy area of Moraine Park, at each long step we place a radar unit on the ground, send a pulse of energy down a few feet, and record the reflections that bounce back. Our intent is to map the depth and type of sediment underlying the meadow. We particularly want to know how much sediment the most recent glacier left here and how much has accumulated since the glacier retreated.

This is the unending quest of the geologist: to somehow perceive what we cannot directly observe. All forms of life exist on the thinnest skin of the planet. Earth's crust thickens to 40 miles under mountains and thins to only 3 miles in parts of the ocean basins. Below the crust is the mantle, which, at 1,800 miles thick,

A view west from Moraine Park, with the Big Thompson River in the foreground.

constitutes the vast majority of Earth's mass. Below the mantle is another 2,160-mile thickness of rock and magma in the core. We can only metaphorically scratch our heads about most of Earth's interior. Like a beachcomber trying to guess the nature of the ocean's interior from shells and dead sea creatures stranded on the beach by a receding tide, geologists can look at rocks brought up from deep in the mantle by volcanic eruptions or mountain building. Any inferences that we may draw from these rocks are constrained by lack of direct knowledge, but we have come a very long way in being able to draw inferences.

Rocks chronicle their own history. Sedimentary rocks formed closer to Earth's surface have bedding that reflects whether the sediment was deposited in a desert sand dune, a marsh, a river, or the deep sea. Metamorphic and igneous rocks formed at greater depths record their history in the size and composition of their crystals and the isotopic ratios of their elements. Isotopes are two or more forms of the same element that differ in the number of neutrons in their nuclei and thus in their atomic mass. Once radioactive isotopes were discovered by Marie and Pierre Curie and others at the very end of the nineteenth century, geologists quickly realized the potential for determining how long ago a rock had become a rock by cooling from magma in Earth's interior. Over the course of the twentieth century, one isotopic pair after another was applied to geologic dating. Apart from giving rise to a lot of bad jokes in introductory geology classes, geologic dating revolutionized understanding of Earth history and allowed geologists to look down their noses at physicists.

Geologists, extrapolating from observed rates of contemporary geologic processes, had for decades contended that Earth must be quite old. Nobel laureate William Thomson, also known as Lord Kelvin, ridiculed geologic inferences and in 1862 published calculations demonstrating that Earth could be at most 400 million years old based on the amount of time it would take for a planet of Earth's size to cool to its present near-surface temperature. The fly in Kelvin's ointment was that he did not know about convection within the mantle, which moves heat from the interior toward the near-surface, or about radioactive decay, which proceeds at a merry pace in Earth's interior and generates plenty of heat to keep the planet vibrant. (Although 400 million years old might seem quite old enough to most people, we now estimate the age of Earth at 4.5 billion years.)

Radioactive elements such as uranium or argon decay very, very slowly. Approximately 4.47 billion years are required for half of the radioactive uranium (^{238}U) in a rock to decay. As long as magma is present, daughter isotopes that result from the decay can diffuse into the surroundings. Once a mineral or rock cools below the so-called closure temperature, however, the parent and daughter isotopes are locked in place within the mineral or rock. By measuring the rate at which the parent decays to the daughter isotope, the ratio of the two isotopes can be used to determine how long a time has passed since the rock solidified. Rocks seldom have a straightforward history.

Instead, a particular rock can undergo numerous episodes of heating and cooling. Individual minerals within the rock can have closure temperatures ranging anywhere from 536°F to more than 1,832°F, so the population of minerals can record the thermal evolution of the rock over very long time periods.

Another way to connect what you can see on the surface to what you cannot see in the subsurface is to create geologic maps. These maps depict the vertical layering of rock units by extrapolating between isolated outcrops of rock at the surface. England's William Smith created the first geologic map in 1799, expanding the map to all of Britain in 1815. Now it is easy to find online a generalized geologic map of any US state, as well as more detailed maps of smaller spatial areas. But the first geologic maps were a remarkable new tool that allowed miners and engineers, as well as geologists, to connect the surface patches of rock outcrops and understand how the seemingly isolated patches represented undulating or broken layers of rock that alternately rose up into cliffs and plunged into the hidden subterranean.

The third arrow in the geologist's quiver when hunting the hidden is to physically penetrate Earth and pull up sediment or rock to examine directly. I do this on the smallest, but not least strenuous, scale every time I risk the functioning of my spine and my back muscles by pounding a soil corer perhaps three or four feet down and then laboring to pull it up again from the tenacious black clay of a filled beaver pond. Larger budgets and an arsenal of heavy equipment can achieve much more: the deepest well, the Kola Superdeep Borehole, in 1989 reached 40,320 feet down on the Kola Peninsula in Siberia.

A fourth technique to examine the hidden is to send some kind of energy pulse into the ground. Again, I work at the feeble end of the scale, sending little seismic pulses downward by pounding a small metal plate with a sledge hammer, or pulsing radar down a few feet. At the powerful end of the spectrum are the natural signals generated by movements along geologic faults, which manifest at the surface as earthquakes, or artificial signals generated by Vibroseis trucks towing steel plates that are vibrated as they move, or by dynamite. These signals can penetrate up to 60 miles into the crust and are used for oil exploration, as well as studying the internal structure of the planet. This type of imaging takes large budgets and extensive coordination among many people. To borrow a phrase from a colleague who uses beavers as part of stream restoration, my work with hammer seismic or ground-penetrating radar is cheap and cheerful. And cheerful I am on this March morning in Moraine Park.

This is an invigorating day to be outdoors. The air is cold, but the sun is noticeably farther north than it was two months ago. The sunlight reflects blindingly from the scattered patches of snow present in the broad meadow, and the ground remains frozen hard beneath our feet. We have only to lift our eyes upward from the frozen ground to see a panorama of snow-covered peaks beneath the intensely blue sky. Standing beside the Big Thompson River, I look across the meadow to where the golden oranges and grays of the grasses and willow thickets give way to darker green conifer forest at the entrance to Forest Canyon. This canyon is the heart of the Rocky Mountain backcountry and one of the least accessible regions in the national park. From the downstream end of Moraine Park, the canyon creates a broad, forested trough stepping gently upward to the west.

In the Time of Ice

The trough shape of Forest Canyon reflects the glacial history here, as does the name Moraine Park. A large valley glacier flowed down the canyon, fed by tributary glaciers coming primarily from the south down Hayden Gorge, Spruce Canyon, and Fern Creek. A shaded relief map of the park reveals the smaller trough carved by each of these glaciers. At the height of the most recent Pleistocene glaciations approximately 18,000 years ago, the ice was about 500 feet thick when it reached Moraine Park. This would have been an amazing sight: a wall of ice variegated with the azure blue of pure, dense ice; the milky white of bubbled ice; and the gray of sediment-laden ice. Contemporary glaciers provide an indication of how Moraine Park must have looked between about 30,000 and 15,000 years ago, when the ice front ended at the park and melted into streams turbid with sediment that braided a complicated skein of channels and bars across the broad valley floor before concentrating into the narrow canyon of the Big Thompson. What today's glaciers lack is the intriguing animals that lived around the Pleistocene ice front.

Snowmass is a small town located about 100 miles southwest of Rocky Mountain National Park. In 2011, construction activities in Snowmass exposed the buried shoreline of a small glacial lake. Scientists were given a window of a few months to excavate as much as they could of the skeletal remains found along the shoreline. Hurried excavations revealed that the Pleistocene environment around Snowmass alternated through time between tundra and forest. What seem almost fantasy creatures inhabited this lost world: mammoths, mastodons, giant bison, camels, ground sloths, and giant beavers, all animals no longer present in North America, as well as the larger ancestors of contemporary bison and beavers. Truly, there are giants in the earth.

As the climate grew warmer and the glaciers retreated, the giants died off. Mammoths, mastodons, camels, and giant bison were replaced by today's elk, bighorn sheep, bison, and mule deer. Scientists do not agree on the cause of this loss of the big animals, which occurred across North America. Some attribute the change primarily to the warmer climate. Others think the sudden invasion of North America by hunters from Asia decimated the populations of the big animals. Perhaps the combined effects of changing climate and human hunting provided the coup de grâce. Whatever the cause, the species of animals inhabiting North America changed dramatically.

The Pleistocene animals that lived in Snowmass would also have walked here, where I stand admiring the view and listening to the ping of the radar unit. A herd of elk do not really substitute for the ancient giants, but the marks left on the landscape by glaciers make it easier to imagine conditions during the time of ice. Two long, steep-sided ridges covered in conifer forest surround Moraine Park like the head of a pair of pliers. These are the lateral moraines, enormous linear ridges of sediment dropped from melting ice along the sides of the glacier. A slight rise at the downstream end of Moraine Park marks the position of the terminal moraine, a mound of sediment deposited across the down-valley end of the glacier, perpendicular to the trend of the valley.

For reasons scientists don't yet understand, glaciers typically retreat in a punctuated rhythm. The ice front remains at one location for decades, abruptly retreats a few hundred feet up-valley, then again remains stable for decades. An end moraine of sediment records the position of the ice front during each stable period, and the terminal moraine indicates the farthest advance down-valley.

I study the lateral moraine across the meadow, trying to understand just how much sediment can be carried by a mass of ice 500 feet thick. I have seen active glaciers in Alaska and Greenland and what strikes me most forcefully about the front of a glacier is the immense wall of ice that can glow with an intense blue as though lit from inside. Yet once the glacier retreats, it is the huge piles of sediment left behind that I find amazing. Memories of active glaciers help me understand how the comparatively small glaciers once present here around Moraine Park created the impressive ridge I now face.

A paradox of glacial history in Rocky Mountain National Park is that the thick masses of Pleistocene ice, able to create landscapes that have persisted for 15,000 years, were nonetheless small relative to valley glaciers elsewhere in the world. The Big Thompson glacier flowed about 14 miles before ending in Moraine Park. The Poudre glacier, the largest in the area, flowed about

25 miles. By comparison, the glaciers of Washington's Olympic Mountains made it all the way from the crest of the range down beyond the mountain front and into the adjacent lowlands, a distance of more than 40 miles along some valleys. The limiting factor in the Colorado Front Range, during the Pleistocene and now, is moisture. The Front Range was sufficiently cold during the Pleistocene, but it was still a long way from the Pacific Ocean or any other source of the plentiful precipitation needed to feed a really large glacier. The glaciers on the western side of the national park were a little larger, and the corresponding glacial lakes, moraines, and valleys that they created are a little more substantial.

The terminal moraine at Moraine Park is barely noticeable today, perhaps in part because of modifications associated with construction of Bear Lake Road. The road follows the moraine, forming a slightly elevated platform from which to view the expanse of mountains to the west. Although the Big Thompson River has cut a notch into the moraine, the glacial sediment still creates a barrier upstream of which the river has deposited its own sediment over thousands of years, forming the broad, flat meadow of today. Beavers have been an important part of the history of building this meadow.

Enter the Beavers

Each of the valley parks on the eastern side of the national park—Moraine Park, Hollowell Park, and others—was once the site of an extensive beaver meadow. A beaver meadow is a complex maze of branching and rejoining channels, ponds, wet meadows, and willow thickets that form where beavers construct dams across a broad valley bottom. As long as beavers maintain the dams, snowmelt peak flows are forced out of the main channel and across the valley bottom. Water flowing over the floodplain cuts secondary channels and soaks into the ground, sustaining wetlands. Yearling beavers strike out on their own, building new dams up- or down-valley. A mated pair abandons one lodge and builds a new one elsewhere along the stream. The pond behind each dam gradually fills with sediment. With time, the valley bottom becomes a mosaic of water and vegetation that I find challenging to walk across.

Ecologists estimate that beavers colonized valley bottoms newly uncovered by retreating glaciers within 2,000 years after the ice melted. I imagine the hardy beaver pioneers, gazing from the shoulder of the lateral moraine across the valley of the Big Thompson River, studying the lush willow thickets, and deciding that this is the place. As far as we can tell, beavers remained in the larger valleys of Rocky Mountain National Park for the next 13,000 years, damming streams and periodically establishing new colonies a short distance up- or down-valley. In the process, the beavers created a mosaic of habitats for rushes and sedges, grasses, wildflowers, willows, river birch, alders, and aspen, not to mention frogs and waterfowl in the ponds, songbirds migrating through, river otters along the streams, or moose browsing the willows. Glaciers sculpted the foundation of each valley and then the beavers moved in and decorated the valley bottoms with life. Along with the beaver dams, the riverside forests slowed the current of flood waters spilling out of the channel across the floodplain, allowing sediment to settle onto the valley floor and then be bound into place by the densely intertwined roots of willows. Glaciers, beavers, and riverside plants acted as partners in creating the landscape architecture that forms such a perfect view from Moraine Park.

To my eyes, however, the view is incomplete because it lacks beaver dams and wet meadows. Beavers have disappeared from most of the beaver meadows within the park only during the past few decades, but their loss has markedly changed the valley bottoms. As the dams fell into disrepair after the beavers vanished, snowmelt peak flows remained within the main channel. The energetic flows, unhindered by beaver dams, eroded the stream banks and enlarged the channel, so that water stopped flowing into secondary channels. In the absence of flood waters spreading across the valley bottom and filtering into the sediment, the water table dropped and the beaver ponds gradually filled with sediment or dried out. Elk and moose browsed the willows heavily and many of the willows died back to the roots. The meadow in Moraine Park became a drier grassland across which we now walk easily. Along the edges of this drier valley we see new pioneers—seedling pines—establishing a roothold. If this continues, the grassland will become a pine forest.

We are using ground-penetrating radar here because we want to understand how much sediment has accumulated behind beaver dams through time. Sediment fills abandoned beaver ponds and plants grow over the surface, obscuring the work of the beavers. But where the dams are close to the surface, we can easily identify them by the abrupt step down in the valley bottom below the dam and by the gnawed pieces of wood protruding from the soil and plants. By imaging these dams and ponds with radar, we can identify the characteristic appearance of pond sediments in the reflected radar waves and use this "signature" to search for more deeply buried beaver ponds and dams. We seek to understand the natural range of variability in Moraine Park when beavers were present—how much sand and silt accumulated over time behind the beaver dams and how rates of accumulation varied over thousands of years—and how these processes have changed as beavers disappeared.

When my students and I analyze the data from our ground-penetrating radar surveys across Moraine Park during the weeks to come, we learn that filled beaver ponds account for about half of the sediment that has accumulated in the broad valley since the glaciers retreated. My respect for the ability of beavers to modify landscapes grows substantially.

How Long Is Eternity?

The desire to understand rates of sediment accumulation over thousands of years brings us up against the other great challenge of geology: to measure ages of sediment and rock and rates of geologic processes. Geologists studying landscape evolution over hundreds of millions of years have their isotopes—uranium, argon, helium, and such. Those of us focusing on the more recent history of Earth—the last 2 million years of geologic time known as the Quaternary—have a different array of techniques that cover much shorter time spans. Until about the 1980s, the only isotopic technique available to Quaternary geologists was radiocarbon dating. All living organisms have radioactive carbon-14 in their tissues in quantities that are in equilibrium with the amount of carbon-14 in the atmosphere. Once an organism dies, carbon-14 steadily decays into the stable carbon-12 isotope at a rate such that about half of the carbon-14 disappears every 5,730 years. This means that radiocarbon dating can only be used on bones, shells, wood, or charcoal younger than about 80,000 years, and of course the sediment being dated must contain some type of dead organism's remains.

Starting in the 1980s, the diversity of dating methods available to Quaternary geologists expanded enormously. If you seek to understand the chronology of events in Earth history, radioactive decay provides a marvelous tool with numerous isotopes that decay over time periods short and long. The challenge has been to understand how and where those isotopes accumulate, to find an isotope with a rate of decay that makes it applicable to the time span of interest, whether events during the 10,000 years of the Holocene or the more than 4 billion years of Earth history, and to figure out how to use the ratios of that isotope to infer geologic processes. Three forms of radioactive decay—in addition to radiocarbon—are especially useful for Quaternary geology: cosmogenic isotopes, luminescence, and bomb isotopes.

The use of cosmogenic isotopes began when scientists realized that isotopic ratios within some minerals at the surface of rock outcrops changed in response to exposure to solar radiation. Break off the upper inch of the rock, grind it into powder, and measure the isotopic ratios, and you can infer how long that cliff face or large boulder has been standing, undisturbed, at the surface. This freed Quaternary geologists from always having to find some remnant of living tissue in association with rock or sediment. Finding buried wood or bone fragments can be extraordinarily difficult among the giant boulders left by a rockfall that occurred thousands of years earlier, but cosmogenic isotopes that began to accumulate in the newly exposed cliff face from which the rocks fell, or in the large boulders that were abraded as they fell, can reveal the time elapsed since the rockfall.

Luminescence developed as a new dating tool when archeologists realized they could determine how long ago a clay pot was fired. Naturally occurring radioactive elements such as uranium continually fire off subatomic particles as the element decays. These silent, invisible explosions leave a record in energy stored within surrounding grains of sand and clay. When the sand and clay are formed into a pot and heated, the stored energy is released. Once the pot cools, the particles of clay begin to accumulate energy once more. Archeologists can take fragments of the pot, heat them, measure the energy released, and infer the length of time since the pot was fired. For fired clay, heating releases accumulated energy and recooling of the fired pot seals the clay particles and allows them to once again accumulate energy. For sediment in desert dunes or river bars, exposure to solar radiation releases accumulated energy when wind and water transport the sand and clay at the surface. Burial allows the sand and clay to once again accumulate energy. Collect buried sediment and shield it from sunlight, take it back to a laboratory and heat it above the Curie point, measure the energy released, and you can estimate how long that sediment has been buried. Having spent many hours carefully sifting through river sediments in a sometimes futile search for charcoal, I felt as though luminescence dating freed me from the tyranny of finding suitable material for radiocarbon dating.

The third tool in moving beyond radiocarbon dating for

Quaternary geology came to us courtesy of the Cold War. Nuclear bomb tests during the 1950s and 1960s released a suite of new, relatively short-lived radioactive isotopes that diffused nearly instantaneously (by geologic timescales) throughout the planet's atmosphere, soil, water, and living organisms. Now, if a laboratory test reveals cesium-137 in sediment, the sediment was deposited after 1950 and the specific concentrations of these bomb isotopes may indicate when after 1950.

Cosmogenic isotopes, luminescence dating, and bomb isotopes broadened the horizons of geologists studying recent Earth history. These techniques allowed us to measure the age of sediments deposited decades ago, or hundreds of thousands of years ago, as well as rock surfaces and sediments that did not contain dead organisms. Thinking about our ability to infer deep Earth history from the isotopic ratios in a mineral and to work out the chronology of glacial advance and retreat from the atmospherically influenced isotopes present in the upper inch or two of bedrock, a pair of quotes comes to mind. William Blake's "To see the world in a grain of sand and hold eternity in the palm of your hand" encapsulates the eons of time and continental-scale changes that a sand grain can reveal. E. O. Wilson's "The ideal scientist thinks like a poet and only later works like a bookkeeper" exemplifies the ingenuity and creativity of the many scientists who contributed to breakthroughs in geologic dating.

Perception and Desire

A sharp March breeze picks up. We take a break from our work to put on wind-resistant jackets and to answer the questions of some curious park visitors out to photograph the elk that frequent Moraine Park. The idea that this valley was once covered in glacial ice surprises them. Most visitors likely don't imagine a Pleistocene world of glaciers and mammoths when they look west toward the continental divide from Moraine Park, the name of the park notwithstanding. What each visitor perceives and imagines has changed with time and these perceptions both shape and reflect park management.

Today most of us think of national parks as environmental preserves designed to protect natural ecosystems. National parks were originally conceived very differently, however, as traced in detail in Richard Sellars's fascinating history, *Preserving Nature in the National Parks: A History*. For much of the history of the national park system, individual units have been managed primarily by people trained in landscape architecture and tourism, who emphasize the visitor experience. Visitor access by road and trail has been designed around scenic viewpoints and recreation, rather than around preserving native ecosystems or emphasizing natural processes such as wildfire that shape these ecosystems. This helps to explain why wildfire was considered a disaster for most of the history of the national parks. Wildfires were wasteful and dangerous events that ruined the scenery for decades.

Understanding this history provides context for past decisions that now seem to contradict the intent of national parks. Before Rocky Mountain National Park was established, homesteaders built cabins and tourist lodges in Moraine Park and used the meadows as cattle pasture. Existing ranches and resorts were not removed until the 1960s and a few private inholdings remain along the edge today. A nine-hole golf course was built in Moraine Park in connection with one of the resorts and the final traces of the course were not removed until 2009. The National Park Service blasted out boulders and cleared brush near Fern Lake, just upstream from Moraine Park, to create ski and sledding runs around the lake in the early 1920s. Hidden Valley had extensive timber harvest and a sawmill from the 1880s to early 1900s, and then a ski course with chairlifts from 1934 to 1992. Roads, campgrounds, and trails continue to be built in national parks to enhance visitor access, but the intensive landscape engineering for recreational activities not directly tied to the mission of the national parks is unlikely to occur today.

I find the shift in attitudes toward wildlife particularly interesting. Predators including foxes, coyotes, martens, mountain lions, and bobcats were actively shot and trapped in the national park until at least 1922 in accord with the prevailing view that these animals were evil at worst and at best ate too many of the charismatic elk and deer that visitors expected to see. This negative view of predators was not unique to park visitors: eminent ecologists such as Aldo Leopold once held similar views. My mother told me of visiting Rocky Mountain National Park during the 1950s and seeing animal furs for sale in the visitor center gift shop. The attitude toward predators did not begin to change until the 1960s and 1970s. Several factors probably caused the change in attitudes. Scientific studies showed the ecological importance of predators, and predators began to be portrayed more positively in the media. Increasing urbanization also shifted attitudes regarding the natural world from consumptive to more protective.

None of us enters a national park as *tabula rasa*. We enter brimming over with the prevailing attitudes of our society and our period in history. This "we" includes the park service personnel charged with managing the national parks. Attitudes change with time. Increasing human population density and use of natural resources have changed nineteenth-century perceptions of the United States as a limitless storehouse of timber, fertile soil, clean water, and huntable fish, birds, and animals, to twenty-first-century perceptions of a fragile, endangered natural world vanishing beneath a tidal wave of humanity and pavement. Scientific research has altered early twentieth-century perceptions of predators as cruel villains to early twenty-first-century perceptions of these species as a critical component of a functioning, healthy ecosystem and as beautiful animals that enrich the experience of a park visitor lucky enough to catch a glimpse of one. Similarly, scientific research has reversed the idea that all wildfires are catastrophes that destroy healthy forests, to the idea that fires sometimes provide a critical disturbance that maintains diverse, healthy, resilient forests.

Our values and desires inevitably accompany us into the national parks, individually and as a society, and govern our responses to the natural environment, our understanding of what we see around us, and our management of the national parks. The dramatic changes in the appearance and function of Moraine Park through time reflect geologic and climatic changes over tens of thousands of years, but also changes in human attitudes over the past century. I imagine viewing Rocky Mountain National Park first like a telescope that includes long times and large extents, and then focusing in like a microscope on progressively shorter times and smaller distances. The view would reveal the ecosystems within the park continually changing in response to varied rhythms:

Geologic rhythms from the movement of Earth's tectonic plates that build mountains.

  Climatic rhythms of changes in solar radiation that drive glaciers.

    Weather rhythms of wildfires and rainfall that structure upland forests and rivers.

      Human-altered rhythms from suppressing wildfires, killing predators, promoting ski lifts, or building roads.

I view Moraine Park as a geologist conscious of the geologic processes that shape landscapes and as a geomorphologist striving to understand the natural rhythms of the park during the past few centuries. The broad valley in which I stand admiring the mountains exists because a Pleistocene glacier did not have enough mass to flow farther down-valley and deposited a terminal moraine here. The moraine across the lower valley helped to trap water and sediment, creating a wet valley bottom in which beavers built dams. The beaver dams trapped sediment moving down the river during the millennia after the glacier retreated, creating a fertile environment for the aspen and willow on which elk like to graze.

The scenery and the wildlife inspired the creation of a national park that now draws millions of visitors from around the world.

I also recognize how humans have altered natural rhythms during the past century. The resorts, golf course, and grazing destroyed the beaver meadow. The removal of predators and the subsequent increase in elk populations limited the recovery of willows and aspens that elk like to graze, and the lack of food and dam-building materials constrained the return of beavers to Moraine Park. Now the National Park Service reduces elk numbers and builds fences to keep the elk from grazing riverside trees, with the hope of eventually reintroducing beavers to the valley bottom. At whatever scale I consider, the view west from Moraine Park is layered with meaning.

April
Lily Lake: Animal Rhythms

Lily Lake is cupped by mountains. To the north stand Lily
Mountain and Rams Horn Mountain, southeast are the Twin
Sisters, and southwest is Estes Cone, overshadowed at a distance
by the massive shape of Longs Peak. Winter continues at the rocky
heights, but here at the edge of the lake, spring has clearly arrived.
Wind-drifted snow lies crusted against the lake edges and hikers
have compacted the snow along the trail into thick, dense ice,
but meltwater stands puddled on the ice at the center of the lake.
Pasque flowers bloom along the snow-free, south-facing slopes
above the lake. The steadily lengthening days have a teasing warmth
at their core before plunging back below freezing each night.

There will be nights during the height of summer when the
temperature here will dip below freezing. At 8,900 feet elevation,
Lily Lake is a vertical midway point within Rocky Mountain
National Park. Subalpine spruce and fir forest surround the
lakeshore, but I can clearly see timberline and the scree slopes
and tundra meadows of the higher elevations around Longs Peak.
Turning to the northeast, where the outlet of Lily Lake into Fish
Creek now lies hidden beneath a thick snow bank, I can see how
the landscape folds between the Twin Sisters and Lily Mountain,
funneling broadly down the Fish Creek valley to Estes Park and Big
Thompson Canyon, in the montane zone of pine forests.

Lily Lake perches at the edge of the subalpine and montane
forests more obviously than other sites along the national park
boundary because of the abrupt drop down to the Fish Creek
valley. Although some animals such as pikas are found largely in
a single elevation zone, many other species migrate between the
zones either seasonally or during some portion of their life. The
arbitrary boundaries of the national park have influenced these
animal rhythms for a century.

Classifications and Complexity

From a vantage point on the edge of the lake, the usefulness of organizing plant and animal communities based on elevation is clear. I know that I can only find the outsize white flowers of arctic gentian above timberline, and the intricate pink blooms of fairy slipper orchids are most common near streams in the subalpine zone. Scientists have noted for centuries that plant and animal communities vary in relation to climate and that climate varies in relation to elevation and latitude. German explorer and scientist Alexander von Humboldt recognized such zonation during his travels in South America between 1799 and 1804. He delineated lines of equivalent temperature that could be used to compare climates among continents and to recognize trends with latitude and altitude.

The penchant of scientists to make sense of the world's complexity by developing classification systems has a long history. Classical Greek philosophers divided matter into earth, water, air, fire, and aether. Swedish scientist Carl Linnaeus published a classification system for plants and animals called *Systema Naturae* in 1735, which gave rise to the contemporary classification of genus and species.

The scientific tendency to categorize and classify accelerated during the nineteenth century. Perhaps this was the product of a collision between the Victorian expectation of orderly and rational progress and the increasing need to psychologically control the vast amounts of new information revealed by undertakings as diverse as polar exploration and newly discovered radioactive elements. The nineteenth century bequeathed us methods for classifying types of rocks and for ordering the surface distribution of those rocks in geological maps (William Smith, 1815); a scheme for ordering the elements in a periodic table (Dmitri Mendeleev, 1869); and evolutionary schemes for living organisms (Charles Darwin, 1859) and for landscapes (William Morris Davis, 1889).

In the midst of this great ordering of the natural world, C. Hart

Golden-mantled ground squirrel (Callospermophilus lateralis) *at Lily Lake. These ground squirrels are common in the park and throughout the mountains of the western United States.*

Merriam proposed in 1889 that the distribution of small mammals across North America, which he had been studying for years, coincided with zones defined by temperature and precipitation. Specifically, Merriam proposed that changes in animal communities with an increase in latitude at a constant elevation are similar to changes that occur with an increase in elevation at a constant latitude. In other words, I could observe similar changes in plant and animal species as I climbed from Lily Lake to the summit of Longs Peak, or as I drove hundreds of miles north from Lily Lake but maintained the same elevation.

Merriam's classification scheme was most widely used in the western part of the continent. He distinguished six life zones: Lower Sonoran, Upper Sonoran, Transition, Canadian, Hudsonian, and Arctic-Alpine. The system was initially very popular, but it is seldom used today. Although the underlying premise is sound, Merriam painted with brushstrokes too broad. The chaparral vegetation of the Upper Sonoran zone, for example, consists of very different plant and animal species in Arizona and Nevada. Ecologists still refer to zonation of natural communities by elevation, but the designations are more detailed and specific to individual regions in which the distributions of plants and animals have been carefully mapped. Merriam's life zones also fell from favor because scientists at one time thought that groups of plant and animal species stayed together, moving to higher elevations or latitudes during periods of warmer climate and then to lower elevations or latitudes during glacial cooling. Careful study of fossil records has discredited this idea. Species that share geographic ranges today have not necessarily been so cozy throughout their existence and have commonly shifted their ranges at different rates and in different directions in response to changing climate.

The world is commonly not as tidy as we would like it to be. Every scientist knows this, but a fundamental tension underlies the need to seek patterns and consistency among the incredible diversity of the world and the need to remain aware of and open to the insights that can result from recognizing diversity. Balanced between these, we impose arbitrary boundaries on the natural continuum as a way to make sense of the complexity. But boundaries and classifications are not just artificial constraints that scientists impose for convenience: classifications of natural phenomena both reflect and direct understanding. Linnaeus recognized that mating robins produce always and only more robins, and he assigned robins a genus and species that reflects their degree of similarity to sparrows as well as to tigers. Darwin did not know of genes or chromosomes, but he understood that something occurring during the mating of robins could eventually result in offspring that were not exactly robins, although they were closely related. This recognition led Darwin to explore the evidence that new species arose from existing species.

Contemporary ecologists recognize elevation zones within Rocky Mountain National Park in the designation of alpine, subalpine, and montane zones, each of which has characteristic plant and animal species. These zones reflect our understanding of plants and animals and also direct us to ask questions about how the distributions of individual species have changed in response to human settlement of the region and will continue to change as climate grows warmer.

Room to Move

Plants and animals must have flexibility to respond to disturbances such as wildfire or climate change. A key component of this flexibility comes from room to move. Any isolated population of a plant or animal is vulnerable. Spontaneous genetic mutations that continually arise in all organisms can sometimes confer an advantage but often do not. In a large population of interbreeding individuals, negative mutations can be effectively damped out, but in a small, relatively inbred population, the mutations may persist and weaken the ability of organisms to survive.

Small populations are also vulnerable to disturbances. A wildfire could destroy all the individuals in one population of the delicate white twinflowers that I so enjoy seeing in the moist understory of subalpine forest. If other populations of twinflowers exist in the surrounding area, the burned zone could be recolonized by seeds blown in on the wind or carried in on the feet of birds or the fur of mammals.

Room to move thus involves genetic exchange with other populations and the potential to recolonize a site via transported seeds or migrating individuals after a population is destroyed. Room to move can also involve migrations over shorter and longer periods. The shortest of movements are those made on a daily basis to find food and avoid predators. Both aquatic and terrestrial creatures commonly forage at night and seek shelter during the day.

Sometimes, when I lie down in my tent after a long day of fieldwork during which I have seen relatively little wildlife, I think about the fact that the active period is just starting for many animals. Usually, it's a brief thought, however, before I fall into sleep like a rock dropped from a cliff.

Animals move to find mates and to avoid predators. Smaller individuals may move to avoid areas dominated by larger, territorial adults or dominant individuals. I witnessed a striking example of this at Brooks Falls in Alaska's Katmai National Park. I visited the park during the late July salmon migration, when the region's grizzly bears parceled out the hours of continuous daylight among themselves. Younger bears or females with cubs scooped the large, pink-fleshed fish from the clear water during the day, but left well before the older males arrived in the evening. The timing of animal movements varies by species and life stages, but animals in the streams, lakes, forests, and tundra are always on the move to some degree.

Short migrations are undertaken by individuals in response to seasonal or episodic changes. Left to their own devices, elk migrate to higher meadows during the summer and then move down to a winter range. Elk also migrate to greener pastures along creeks during a sustained drought. In each scenario, elk populations thrive only where they have the room to migrate as necessary under changing conditions.

Longer migrations can reflect progressively changing climate. Many species have unique physiological or behavioral adaptations that allow them to survive under specific conditions. Because of their distinctive blood chemistry and unusually thick feathers, ouzels can move underwater seeking food in cold mountain streams. These birds cannot survive in warmer waters. Similarly, the thick fur and round bodies of pikas preserve heat during winter in the alpine zone, but the animals can overheat and die when exposed to temperatures of 78°F and higher. As the climate warms, individual populations of ouzels and pikas must be able to migrate upward or northward to suitable habitats, or they will go extinct.

Rocky Mountain National Park is a protected island of natural habitats surrounded by a sea of human alteration. And, just like the real oceans of the world, the metaphorical sea of human alteration is rising. Elk herds in the park move down to winter ranges in what is now the city of Estes Park, where gardeners do not appreciate elk browsing their trees and shrubs. Although the elk can and do wander into Estes Park, because of human disturbances outside the park the elk likely spend a disproportionate amount of time within the national park in what would normally be only summer range. The elk also appear to have learned not to stray into the adjacent national forests frequented by hunters.

From an ecosystem perspective, Rocky Mountain National Park is truncated on the eastern side by the lack of natural meadows in Estes Park as winter range for elk and as habitat for beavers. In the dark, rich topsoil exposed in cutbanks along Fish Creek within Estes Park, I see the ghost of beaver meadows past. But homeowners along Fish Creek do not want their lots submerged beneath beaver ponds or their riverside aspen forests felled by beaver teeth.

If Rocky Mountain National Park had been delineated by contemporary ecologists free to ignore private property, the park boundaries would extend down at least one major canyon to the base of the mountains. Such a dream park would include the full range of plant and animal communities of the Colorado Front Range: alpine tundra, subalpine spruce and fir forest, montane ponderosa pine forest, and chaparral of juniper, pinyon pines, and woody shrubs such as rabbitbrush. This strategy would have provided a buffer against the increasingly dense development surrounding the park. A larger and more elevationally inclusive park might have provided room for natural ecosystem dynamics, such as migrations of mountain lions between the park and other protected areas, as well as an area large enough to support the wide-ranging wolves and grizzly bears once present in the park.

This is the rationale currently driving environmental protection in the Northern Rockies, where migration corridors are being identified and acquired between major protected areas such as Yellowstone and Glacier National Parks. By developing a Crown of the Continent protected region, ecologists hope to preserve species such as Canada lynx, gray wolves, and fishers well into the future by allowing individual populations of these animals to interbreed and move as needed in response to wildfires, blizzards, or other hazards.

The dream of such a spatially diverse and extensive protected area around Rocky Mountain National Park is ecological fantasy. The national park was established long after private property was entrenched in the area and, like all of the national parks, was initially designed for scenery and visitor enjoyment, not for ecosystem inclusiveness. Now we must work with what past generations bequeathed us, but that work can be informed by understanding of what went before.

Beaver Colonists

Here at Lily Lake, beavers are a key part of what went before. Many individuals worked to establish Rocky Mountain National Park, but Enos Mills was foremost among them and is usually credited as the father of the park. Mills had a cabin near Lily Lake and spent many hours observing the wildlife in and around the lake. In his 1913 book *In Beaver World*, Mills writes affectionately of the activities of beavers. Mills describes an extensive system of canals the beavers dug in the lake bed so they could move about more easily during dry periods of shallow water. Mills carefully measured the canals, noting with amazement that one canal was 750 feet long and 3 feet deep throughout its length. He writes of what he inferred to be the first beaver to inhabit the lake, in the 1870s, and he describes a later phase of pioneer beavers recolonizing the lake for a time, having been chased upslope from Estes Park by human encroachment.

The next summer a house was built in the lily pads near the shore. Here a number of children were born during the few tranquil years that followed. These times came to an end one bright midsummer day. Lord Dunraven had a ditch cut in the outlet rim of the lake with the intention of draining it that his fish ponds, several miles below in his Estes Park game-preserve, might have water. A drouth had prevailed for several months, and a new water-supply must be had or the fish ponds would go dry. The water poured forth through the ditch, and the days of the colony appeared to be numbered.

A beaver must have water for safety and for the ease of movement of himself and his supplies. . . . The morning after the completion of the drainage ditch, a man was sent up to the lake to find out why the water was not coming down. A short time after the ditch-diggers had departed, the lowering water had aroused the beaver, who had promptly placed a dam in the mouth of the ditch (pp. 179–180).

Mills then describes how the ditch-diggers proceeded to trap or shoot six animals, until the colony gave up: "The lake was drained, and the colonists [beavers] abandoned their homes. One night, a few days after the final attempt to blockade the ditch, an unwilling beaver emigrant party climbed silently out of the uncovered entrance of their house and made their way quietly, slowly, beneath the stars, across the mountain, descending thence to Wind River, where they founded a new colony" (p. 182).

Today the outlet of Lily Lake is heavily stabilized with large boulders and there is little sign that beavers once built dens along the lakeshore. From the outlet, I have a clear view of the enormous stone beaver silhouette pointing its nose up the slope at the rounded top of Longs Peak. Willow thickets remain along portions of the lakeshore and beavers could potentially establish a new colony along the lake, but the park service would likely have to

Beaver lodge along North St. Vrain Creek in Wild Basin.

intervene by removing some of the outlet boulders or limiting the access of elk to the area. I have seen families with young children taking pleasure in the sight of ground squirrels and chipmunks along the trail, as well as ducks in the shallows. I can easily imagine them delighting in the sight of a beaver swimming steadily across the still water, a willow branch clasped in its mouth.

Then, a year after I visited the lake and wrote this chapter, the beavers appear. They come in at the southern end of the lake, where a marsh of willows and sedges had probably been a beaver meadow decades earlier. These are not covert colonists fearing some latter-day Lord Dunraven: their lodge laps over the edge of the trail, forcing people to detour slightly to avoid the protruding wood. Not that the people seem to mind. I have given talks on beavers in the national park and afterward had members of the audience proudly come up to show me photos on their cellphones of the Lily Lake beavers.

With a little imagination, the notch to the left of the summit of Longs Peak resembles the nose of a beaver pointed up toward the summit.

(Whenever I return to the lake, however, the beavers are napping or otherwise unaccountably shy, and I have yet to actually see them.)

The outlook is not necessarily rosy for the Lily Lake colony, however. When I visited during the summer of 2015 the area was in the midst of an outbreak of tularemia. Tularemia is an infectious disease caused by a bacterium that includes several subspecies with varying levels of virulence. The bacterium is spread primarily by ticks and deer flies. The most virulent form affects humans and can be transmitted from rabbits, hares, and pikas. The form that affects beavers and muskrats is less virulent for humans, but can certainly kill the aquatic rodents. During one of my visits I passed a dead muskrat sprawled along the boardwalk on the trail beside the lake, as though the poor little animal had suddenly keeled over while walking along. With luck, at least some of the beavers will survive the outbreak and the new colony will persist.

Suitable habitat may be a greater limitation for the Lily Lake beaver colony over the years to come. Lily Lake is next to the peak-to-peak highway and at the edge of the national park. Although national forest lands abut the park boundary in places, the boundary is ragged with smaller parcels of private land that may or may not be beaver-friendly. In any new colony such as the one at Lily Lake, there is always the possibility that the habitat is what ecologists call a population sink: a site that appeals to the animals but that does not actually have enough food or habitat to sustain a population.

In a world in which human-altered environments dominate most regions, ecologists have developed a subdiscipline known as insular biogeography to explore the minimum area needed to sustain individual populations of diverse plants and animals. Insular biogeography started as island biogeography and focused on actual islands, mostly in oceans. During the 1960s, ecologists Robert MacArthur and E. O. Wilson sought to understand what controlled the diversity of species on these isolated natural communities. They proposed that the number of species on an island reflected some balance between immigration and extinction. Immigration is affected by the distance of the island from a source of colonists. Extinction is affected by island size. Larger islands have larger habitat areas and a greater variety of habitats. Larger habitat areas reduce the probability of extinction due to a natural disaster such as a wildfire or tularemia outbreak, and a greater variety of habitats increases the number of species that can thrive after immigrating. MacArthur and Wilson proposed that the balance between immigration and extinction on an island would eventually create an equilibrium number of species that can be predicted based on the size of the island.

Other ecologists quickly realized that the mathematical models of MacArthur and Wilson can also be applied to the islands of habitat effectively created by farm fields or urban areas that isolate remnants of natural habitat. Viewing relatively small

A new dam at the southern end of Lily Lake (muddy berm on this page) and a lodge lapping onto the trail (opposite page), summer 2015.

national parks, such as Rocky Mountain, through the lens of island biogeography, made some eyebrows shoot up in alarm. Ecologists and environmentalists realized that even relatively large and long-established parks such as Yellowstone might not be quite big enough for large-bodied animals with extensive migration ranges, such as bison. The concern was borne out by a study by William Newark that demonstrated a strong correlation between national park size and the number of species of mammals.

Substantially increasing the size of a national park is an extraordinarily difficult task in much of the United States, so environmentalists turned to the idea of wildlife corridors as a means of increasing the ability of animals to move between habitat islands. This idea underlies the Crown of the Continent region in the northern US Rocky Mountains, for example, in which conservation efforts deliberately target areas that can provide

migration corridors for diverse species. Recognition of the importance of the size of protected areas also led to what David Quammen described as "ecology's own genteel version of trench warfare" in his book *The Song of the Dodo*: a vigorous argument over whether environmental protection should focus on a few very large or many smaller protected areas. Although I don't think smallness of a natural area is a reason to sacrifice it on the brutal altar of "progress," it is crucial to understand that protecting only a limited area of northern hemisphere nesting habitat for a migratory songbird, for example, will not by itself ensure the survival of that bird species.

Here at Lily Lake, at least some beavers have clearly managed to immigrate to the lake margin from a colony elsewhere. These are probably two-year-olds seeking to start their own colony. The ultimate success of the colony will depend on whether the margins of the lake and the surrounding region provide sufficient food and habitat to sustain the animals here and to support their offspring when they in turn move on to new territory.

The Edges of Lily Lake

The National Park Service continued to buy private property, mostly meadows along the margins of Rocky Mountain National Park, after the park was established in 1915. By 1915, however, it was too late to acquire Estes Park, and there is no evidence that anyone ever thought of going all the way down to the base of the mountains. The only possibility left in 1915 for such an extension of the park would have been North St. Vrain Creek. Since 1965 the lower portion of that creek has been submerged beneath Buttonrock Dam and Ralph Price Reservoir. What remains of North St. Vrain Creek is vitally important. This drainage is the longest unaltered mountain tributary in the entire South Platte River watershed. Every other tributary—the Poudre River, Big Thompson River, Boulder Creek, Clear Creek, Bear Creek, and the South Platte itself—has roads, diversions, dams, and cities much farther upstream along its course. Only along the North St. Vrain, which heads in the national park and then flows down through a roadless canyon in the Arapaho-Roosevelt National Forest, do the plants and animals of the Colorado Front Range have a largely intact, albeit narrow, migration corridor between the uplands and the lower elevations of the range.

North St. Vrain Creek also provides a reference site for research such as my own on logjams and channel forms. Only here can I be confident that the patterns I observe do not reflect direct human alterations of the creek such as timber harvest, flow regulation, or road construction. Logjams are noticeably absent from larger streams in the mountainous portion of the South Platte watershed, for example. Is this because the greater flows and wider channels of the larger streams carry wood downstream more readily? Or does the absence of logjams reflect the regular removal of wood to prevent damage to bridges and irrigation intakes or obstacles to whitewater rafting? Because of North St. Vrain Creek, I think the absence of logjams results from greater transport of wood by stream flow in larger rivers. If I did not have North St. Vrain Creek as a reference site, I could not answer this and other questions about how the mountain streams of the Colorado Front Range naturally change downstream.

As I stand on the shore of Lily Lake on this day at the edge of spring, I see a vertical midway point among the elevation bands that help to structure my understanding of the complex natural rhythms of Rocky Mountain National Park. Included among these are the animal rhythms: seasonal rhythms of Wilson's warblers returning to the park after wintering far to the south; life-stage rhythms of two-year-old beavers leaving their natal colony and striking off toward parts unknown to found a new colony; disturbance rhythms of woodpeckers and olive-sided flycatchers moving into forest fragmented by blowdowns or fires; and changing climate rhythms of marmots emerging from hibernation significantly earlier than they did in recent decades. The ability of animals to move to each of these rhythms requires an extent of land that includes higher and lower elevation zones.

Thinking of Enos Mills's descriptions and the dark soils that indicate past beaver meadows downslope, I also see Lily Lake as metaphorically on the edge between different possible trajectories for the future. The lake represents what might have been and what exists today as a result of land ownership boundaries that constrain the rhythms of animal movement. These boundaries also constrain how people and the natural communities of the national park move into the future. The future could be dominated by warmer, drier climate and local extinctions of plants and animals unable to move to suitable new habitat. Or the future might be one of increasing biological richness as management fosters the reintroduction of species now gone from the park and protection of undeveloped land outside the park boundaries preserves habitat and room to move. Human perceptions and desire, both within and outside of the park service, will largely govern which future comes into being.

The trail to Bridal Veil Falls starts gently. Unlike many trails in the park, this one doesn't force me to immediately start scaling the Rocky Mountains (or so some trails can feel). The trailhead is located at the McGraw Ranch, originally homesteaded in 1875 and used primarily as a dude ranch until acquired by the park service in 1988. The cluster of buildings, along with the name Cow Creek, reminds me of the park's recent history and of the land uses that have shaped this region.

By May the creek is running high with snowmelt. Patches of old, crusted snow persist in the deep shade beneath the conifers along the creek, even as the first flowers are starting to bloom on the south-facing slopes above. The trail follows the creek upstream through a broad, open valley. The terrain appears as though it could have been sculpted by Pleistocene glaciers, as in Wild Basin or Moraine Park, but glacial ice never filled this valley. What this valley does have in common with Wild Basin, the Upper Colorado River, Moraine Park, and Lily Lake is that the appearance of the valley today reflects the activities of beavers.

I am here on a warm, sunny day in mid-May to map the beaver dams along the creek. The rhythm of my year is accelerating for the strenuous physical activity of summer field research. While mapping logjams the previous summer, I realized that many of the breached soil berms across the creeks I walked were the remnants of old beaver dams. Intrigued at the large number of these old dams throughout the park, I decided to systematically map them and try to understand whatever story they might tell. Cow Creek has abandoned dams spaced so closely along the valley that the stream must have been mostly ponded water during the era of maximum beaver occupancy.

Ecosystem Engineers

Beavers have received many admiring names because of their skill in building dams: natural engineers, Nature's engineers, and ecosystem engineers. Ecosystem engineer can refer to any plant or animal species that physically modifies its surroundings to create habitat for itself and, inadvertently, for other organisms. Beavers are usually the first species that comes to mind as an ecosystem engineer because of their superlative skill in creating their own habitat by ponding water behind dams.

I listen to Cow Creek flowing swiftly through a channel largely unimpeded by beaver dams. A few older dams overgrown with grasses and woody shrubs remain, but mostly the water moves without interruption through the abandoned beaver meadow. If a beaver stood beside me today hearing what I hear, things would be different.

The sound of running water can trigger an innate urge in beavers to build dams. Anything that comes to hand—or paw—is used to satisfy this urge. I have seen beaver dams that incorporate bowling ball–sized cobbles and a beaver dam that included a full rack of moose antlers. Mostly, dams consist of chewed pieces of wood about the thickness of a finger to a forearm, with plenty of silt and clay plastered among the interwoven pieces of wood. The dam represents a continual work in progress that the beavers must maintain against the relentless movement of water downslope. Sometimes the beavers choose a secondary channel or a tributary entering the side of a valley and build dams that create a pond perched several feet above the main valley floor. Elsewhere, the animals build one dam after another across a stream so that the valley bottom resembles a staircase of beaver ponds.

The work of building and maintaining the dams falls first to the adult female of the colony. The male and the yearlings help her with these tasks, but she is the primary engineer. Knowing this, it amuses me to read nineteenth-century natural history accounts describing the work of "Mr. Beaver" in building the family home.

Mostly the dams are only 2 to 5 feet tall, but they can be extremely long. The largest dams can be seen on satellite imagery, such as one dam 2,800 feet in length in Canada's Wood Buffalo National Park.

In walking across valley bottoms occupied by beavers I have frequently stumbled into the other primary engineering feature that the animals create: canals one-beaver-wide that can be difficult to see among tall grasses and sedges, but are sufficiently deep to thoroughly soak my foot and leg. Despite their ability to waddle about on their hind legs with an armful of mud and wood clasped to the chest while working on a dam, beavers are much more swift and agile in water than on land. Consequently, they dig a network of canals to make it easier to find food and building materials and escape from predators. Beavers typically have underwater entrances to their lodges and bank dens, and the animals excavate holes to maintain air exchange between the den, entrance burrows, and the surface. These holes are difficult to see when I walk in a beaver meadow but are exceptionally effective at trapping my foot.

I know of no other animal—except humans—that so thoroughly modifies the surroundings. Because I work in rivers, the more I learn about beavers, the more fascinated I become. I am succumbing to what Arthur Radclyffe Dugmore in 1914 called "the romance of the beaver" in a book of the same title. I have plenty of company. Descriptions of the animals and their engineering go back to Herodotus, Hippocrates, and Pliny in the ancient world, and scientists today sing the praises of beavers as architects of biodiversity.

The phrase *beaver meadow* was first introduced to scientific writing in a 1938 paper in the journal *Science*, but the name had been in use for many years among people living in New York and New England, and for centuries in England, where "beaver lea" gave rise to the place name (and woman's name) Beverly. A beaver meadow is a maze of new ponds, old ponds gradually filling with sediment, wet meadows that grew where ponds completely filled, and multiple stream channels and beaver canals winding in and out among dams that also wind across the valley bottom in complicated patterns. To walk into an active beaver meadow is to become quickly lost among thickets of densely growing willow, river birch, and aspen. The spatial pattern of the landscape is best understood when seen from above, in an aerial photograph or from the perspective of a nearby, steep-sided ridge.

Not many people willingly walk into such a wetlands because of the difficulty in moving about. I do, because I cannot effectively see important details from a distance. Mapping dams within a beaver meadow is a research task that leaves me grateful for trails. Even chest waders provide only limited protection. Sinking into the organic-rich ooze of the pond bottom remains too easy, as does getting firmly stuck while trying to squeeze among the innumerable willow stems growing on the berm created by a dam. The beaver ponds along Cow Creek can be comfortably viewed from the trail, but the narrowness of the beaver meadow here partly reflects the history of cattle grazing in this valley. Cows like riverside vegetation just as much as beavers do. Although cattle no longer graze here, the effects of their presence linger in the form of grasses rather than willows along the creek.

The more I learn about the history of human manipulation of seemingly natural landscapes, the more suspicious I become that the appearance of any stream I study at least partly reflects past human activity. During the 1950s, for example, the US Forest Service used aerial herbicide spraying to limit woody plants in meadows grazed by cattle. Although the herbicides have not been applied for half a century, some of these creek-side meadows today remain grasslands rather than willow thickets. Even in the absence of herbicides, large numbers of cattle grazing riverside vegetation for years at a time can kill willows and other woody plants by repeatedly eating the plants down to the ground. Cattle have not grazed the beaver meadow along Cow Creek for more than twenty years, but willows and aspen are just starting to recover and the scarcity of these trees probably limits the number of beavers that can survive in this valley.

One beaver can chew down as many as 300 small to medium-sized trees each year. Beavers dine on salads in the summer, when up to half of their diet can consist of forbs and grasses, but the remainder of their food comes from bark and twigs. An adult needs somewhere between 1.5 and 4 pounds of this food daily. A colony of beavers typically includes a mated pair of adults, their yearlings from the previous year, and the kits of the year, which can work out to anywhere from six to twelve animals. Along a favorable stream, colonies can be spaced at just over half a mile apart. Competition for food in the form of intensive grazing by cows, moose, or elk can limit beaver populations and the extent of beaver meadows, a situation that is widespread within Rocky Mountain National Park. As I hike the trail along Cow Creek, I see a beaver meadow that has fallen on hard times, with limited width across the valley bottom and relatively few active dams.

I pause to watch a buck mule deer lying down and chewing his cud in the meadow. The deer's cheeks bulge as though stuffed to bursting and he seems unfazed by my presence. A little farther on, a coyote forages in the meadow. When I first catch sight of it, the coyote is standing head down, wagging its tail like a dog. The animal eats something and continues nosing about in the grass. I admire the coyote's fur, still thick from the winter recently past. As the coyote looks up and sees me, it becomes alert, but not really worried. I resume hiking and the coyote moves slowly into the forest.

Ghosts of Beavers Past

Three miles in, the trail up Cow Creek starts to climb the northern side of the valley toward the topographic exclamation point of Bridal Veil Falls. The trail ends at the falls, but I easily continue upstream along the creek. The small creek is narrowly constrained above the falls, flowing along a course punctuated by logjams and breached, vegetated berms across the creek. These berms are old beaver dams, recognizable as a linear mound perpendicular to stream flow, with grasses and clumps of willows growing from the mound. Sometimes the ends of beaver-gnawed sticks protrude from the mound, particularly where the creek cut through the dam once the beavers abandoned the site. The abandoned dam of one daredevil beaver lies across the creek only 30 feet upstream from the 120-foot drop of Bridal Veil Falls.

I do not know when these dams were built nor if they were all actively maintained at the same time, creating the same type of stair-stepped stream course present downstream from the falls. What I do know is that the same sequence of abandoned beaver dams, one after another along a creek, is present along every major stream I have walked on the eastern side of Rocky Mountain National Park. From Cony Creek at the southern end of the park to the North Fork Big Thompson River and the Cache la Poudre River at the northern end of the park, the riverscapes are haunted by the ghosts of beavers past.

Many of these now-abandoned dams were built in valleys too narrow and steep to support a beaver meadow. While maintained, each dam would have created a small pond and a miniature wet meadow as the pond filled. Only the wider portions of each stream course could support a fully developed beaver meadow. These wider portions mostly coincide with the segment of valley just upstream from the Pleistocene glacial terminal moraine.

Even if not every dam was occupied simultaneously, the hundreds of dams present on the eastern side of the park represent a lot of beavers. I try to imagine what this landscape looked like before the first people of European descent came here to trap beavers in the early 1800s. All of the large parks that are now covered mostly in grasses with a few shrubs and isolated trees— Estes Park, Moraine Park, Hollowell Park, Beaver Meadows, Horseshoe Park—would have looked more like the beaver meadow at Wild Basin today. Each beaver meadow would have had numerous ponds stepped along the valley, with willow thickets and multiple channels branching and rejoining across the valley bottom. The steeper, narrower valleys up- and downstream from each meadow would have held far more standing water because of the small pond upstream from each beaver dam. The beaver meadows would have functioned like thick, wet sponges, absorbing water in ponds and belowground sand and gravel layers during snowmelt runoff and then gradually releasing the stored water during autumn and winter. The transformation of river valleys that occurred with the disappearance of beavers I call the great drying.

This image of a vanished landscape is intriguing because a beaver pond is not just a pool of standing water. By just about any measure, beaver ponds and beaver meadows are ecological hot spots. Compared to other, equivalently sized areas on the landscape, beaver meadows have a greater diversity of plants, from microscopic algae to trees. Studies across the northern hemisphere show that beaver meadows are home to more species of insects and other invertebrates such as mussels or crayfish, as well as fish, amphibians, and reptiles, especially turtles. Waterfowl and other birds as varied as kingfishers, herons, and songbirds use the ponds and willow thickets as habitat. And mammals from mink to moose spend at least some of their time in the wet meadows. Even the bacteria are more diverse in beaver meadows. Diversity means that a greater number of distinct species of that particular type of organism are present, including species that are only present because of the wetlands created by beaver dams and canals. I love exploring the large beaver meadow on North St. Vrain Creek because I find animals that are uncommon elsewhere in Rocky Mountain National Park, from snipe to warblers and wood frogs to moose.

The slowly moving water in beaver ponds and across the floodplains of beaver meadows also encourages deposition of sediment. Trapped along with the sediment is fine-grained organic matter—the leaves, needles, and twigs shed by the vegetation along each stream. This material is rich in nitrogen and carbon that are needed by living organisms. If the organic matter keeps moving down a swiftly flowing mountain creek, there is little opportunity for microbes or aquatic insects to begin to ingest the dead plant material and absorb the nutrients into living tissues. But if the organic matter is trapped even for a few hours, let alone weeks or months, in a beaver pond, then stream organisms can begin to ingest the organic matter and take up the nutrients. Careful measurements by other scientists in beaver ponds across North America have shown greater amounts and availability of nitrogen, carbon, phosphorus, potassium, calcium, magnesium, iron, and other elements vital to living organisms in the ponds than in other portions of the stream environment.

Beaver meadows are the food larders of river ecosystems. The dams trap plant parts shed by upland and riverside forests. The plant parts are buried in accumulating, saturated muck. As I am reminded every time a misstep in a beaver meadow releases the stench of rotten eggs, the lack of oxygen down in the muck limits the presence of microbes that can release nutrients such as carbon and nitrogen in gaseous form back to the atmosphere. The nutrients are stored in the muck of beaver meadows for periods that can extend to thousands of years. But enough of the nutrients remain biologically available at the surface to support the abundance and diversity of plants and animals present in an active beaver meadow.

Environmental Fairy Tales and Complicated Realities

I return downstream along Cow Creek to the main beaver meadow. The remnant meadow is so narrow and the willows so sparse that I can see the beaver dams from the trail and keep my feet dry by mapping from a distance. Even though I appreciate the easy walking in such abandoned beaver meadows, I keep returning to the tangled, wet thickets of the active beaver meadow along North St. Vrain Creek because they are so full of surprises. Sometimes these are dangerous surprises. One year in June I inadvertently got far too close to a moose cow and calf because I did not see or hear them until they suddenly appeared among the willows. The fur on the cow's hackles went up and I retreated as fast as I could while wearing chest waders and stumbling through beaver holes and dense willow stems. Sometimes the surprise is one of delight, as when I came on a pair of otters chattering like birds along the edge of the creek, or of wonder at something as intricate as the chewed ends of sedges that a caddisfly larva shaped into a structure resembling a tiny pagoda.

Now, as I map the locations of the old beaver dams along Cow Creek, I miss these surprises. The meadow still has a narrow band of willows along the creek and I see the lemon-yellow flash of a male warbler moving among the green leaves. But the valley bottom lacks the complexity created by numerous old beaver dams gradually being filled with sediment and marsh plants.

Where have all the beavers gone? Long time passing. Ecologists estimate that, before Europeans entered North America, somewhere between 60 and 400 million beavers occupied the continent from the Alaskan tundra to northern Mexico. Beavers had once been equally abundant in Eurasia, but trapping the animals for their fur has a much longer history on that continent. Once Europeans reached the New World, they began to trap North American beavers with tremendous enthusiasm, continuing in most regions until the species was nearly extinct.

Trappers did not reach the area around Rocky Mountain National Park until after the Lewis and Clark expedition of 1804–1806. Much of the trapping occurred during the 1820s and 1830s. Ceran St. Vrain, of St. Vrain Creek, exemplifies this history. A trapper of French ancestry, he came to Colorado from Missouri in 1824 and worked with Charles and William Bent. As part of their trapping and trading enterprises, St. Vrain and the

In the active beaver meadow of North St. Vrain Creek: a moose cow and calf crossing the creek; a wood frog in an old beaver pond beside the creek (opposite page top); a caddisfly larva's "house" in the beaver pond (opposite page bottom).

Bent brothers established Fort St. Vrain as a fur trading center at the confluence of St. Vrain Creek and the South Platte River in 1837. They abandoned the fort by 1844 as the supply of beaver furs dwindled. John Charles Frémont described the many abandoned beaver lodges and dams that he saw during his 1842 explorations of the area, as well as the lack of evidence of active beaver colonies. Fur trappers needed only twenty years to largely wipe out beavers in the Southern Rockies.

Beaver populations did subsequently recover slightly after trapping largely ceased. Ecologists estimate that 6 to 12 million beavers now inhabit North America and periodic surveys of beaver populations in Rocky Mountain National Park indicate that the animals recovered between the 1880s and 1950s.

Something happened after that. The something is a complicated

story that ecologists are still trying to unravel, but which appears to have some similarities with the old nursery rhyme about Humpty Dumpty, in which "all the king's horses and all the king's men couldn't put Humpty together again."

Current understanding of the story goes this way: top predators, including wolves, grizzly bears, and wolverines, were hunted to extinction in Colorado by about 1920. Elk were also largely eradicated within Rocky Mountain National Park as a result of excessive hunting. Although residents of the area enjoyed a landscape without predators, they missed the presence of elk. Elk were reintroduced to the area from Montana in 1913, and found it good. Why wouldn't the elk enjoy a place where hunting was no longer allowed, predators were largely gone, and park personnel placed salt blocks beside roads to attract elk, deer, and bighorn sheep for easy viewing by visitors? As noted earlier, moose were also introduced into the region around Rocky Mountain National Park and quickly made their way into the park and increased in number.

As signs of overgrazing became increasingly marked by the late 1930s, park naturalists realized that elk and deer populations were exceeding the carrying capacity of the environment. There followed decades of attempts to limit populations in the highly visible environment of a national park. In 1941, a special hunting season along the park's eastern boundary did not result in enough killing, so in 1944 park rangers shot about 300 elk. Live-trapping and transplanting were tried subsequently, along with contraceptives, tall fences to keep elk and deer away from some of the creek-side forests, and more episodes of selective shooting.

Meanwhile, the beaver meadows disappeared. Elk like the succulent plants that grow along streams and, just like domestic cattle or sheep that are left to their own devices, elk that are not kept moving by the presence of predators will spend a large amount of their time along the streams. A herd of 500- to 700-pound elk is very effective at competing with beavers for their mutually preferred food of willows and aspens. Beaver numbers dropped steadily as elk numbers increased during the second half of the twentieth century.

Having learned this history, I knew that I had unconsciously developed a beaver-centric perspective when I was working in the beaver meadow along North St. Vrain Creek one day and came upon the first elk I had ever seen there. My immediate thought was, "The enemy!"

The story of unnaturally large elk herds displacing beavers is not unique to Rocky Mountain National Park. A similar progression through time has been observed at other national parks in the continental United States where predators were hunted to extinction. At some of these national parks, however, the predators have been reintroduced or have reintroduced themselves by migrating in from Canada. Yellowstone National Park is the prime example of this phenomenon and in some ways represents the inverse of the story just described for Rocky Mountain National Park.

Wolves were hunted to extinction in Yellowstone by 1926, elk subsequently flourished, and beaver numbers dropped. With the reintroduction of wolves to Yellowstone in 1995, an interesting recovery began. Scientists excitedly documented how hunting wolf packs kept elk herds on the move, culling the weak or aging elk just as wolf advocates had been describing for many years, improving the health of the elk population and helping to limit the number of animals to a level that the environment could sustainably support. The unexpected bonus appeared along valley bottoms where reduced grazing by elk allowed the renewal of plant communities not seen in decades, including dense willow thickets and stands of aspens. Soon the beavers followed, building dams that caused snowmelt floods to spread across the valley bottoms rather than shooting downstream wholly within a single channel. The higher water levels associated with the beaver meadows kept the water-hungry willows and aspen growing steadily, assuring the supply of beaver food and the continuance of beaver colonies and meadows.

This is a wonderful story. The predators return and the ecosystem comes back into balance, with a place for beavers and all of the abundance and diversity that they support by building dams. Scientific understanding of ecological interactions leads to public awareness of the importance of predators and enlightened management returns more natural riverscapes to the national parks. Except . . . except it's not that simple.

Alternate Rhythms

When beavers abandon a site, their dams fall into disrepair. Decrepit dams no longer effectively block the stream channel and seasonal floods are less likely to spread across the valley bottom. Swift, high flows contained within a single channel are more erosive, widening and deepening the channel and increasing the likelihood that the water will remain within the channel rather than overtopping the banks. Beaver ponds on and beside the main channel drain and the secondary channels go dry. The water table across the valley bottom drops. Wetland plants disappear and the soil dries.

New pioneers move in. Among these are burrowing rodents such as voles and pocket gophers. These rodents eat plants and the ectomycorrhizal fungi that live in soil within the roots of spruce and fir. The trees cannot survive without the fungi, which help the trees to absorb nutrients from the surrounding soil. Burrowing rodents spread the spores of the fungi by excreting the spores in their feces. As the fungi colonize the newly dry soils, spruce and fir can also colonize the site. The upland plant community gradually moves down into the now relatively dry valley bottom, creating what is sometimes called an elk grassland.

Now the soil is on the dry side for willows and aspen and the main stream has cut down below the level of the surrounding grassland. Even if someone dropped off a pair of happily mated beavers and invited them to be fruitful and multiply, the beavers

An abandoned beaver meadow with overgrazed, isolated clumps of willows and a drier valley bottom along which only a single channel flows. This is Upper Beaver Meadows in the national park.

would have a tough time of it. There are not enough of their preferred woody plants to feed the beavers or to provide dam-building materials. The situation is not impossible. Beavers are resourceful. They will build dams out of mud and cobbles and they will eat grasses and conifers, but deciduous woody plants are the most important part of their diet, as demonstrated by an experiment just north of Rocky Mountain National Park.

In 1999, the US Forest Service reintroduced beavers to a site in the Medicine Bow National Forest in southern Wyoming that had once supported them. The meadow had subsequently been heavily grazed by cattle and had no willows, so the Forest Service dropped off cut aspen trees for the beavers to eat. After three years, the supplemental food supply stopped and the beavers vanished.

The Wyoming site, along with some of the valley bottoms in

Yellowstone and in Rocky Mountain National Park, had entered what ecologists call an alternative stable state. This is a little bit like a steeply descending trail that forks to reach two different valleys. Follow one fork far enough and you come to a valley that seems like a perfect camping spot, not least because to return uphill and reach the other valley would require a significant amount of time and energy. Either valley provides a nice destination, but you need to invest enough energy to climb back out of one valley to reach the other.

Alternative stable states describe two possible scenarios for an ecosystem. Either alternative can remain stable for a long period of time, but some major change is required to shift the ecosystem from one alternative to the other. In a wide valley upstream from a terminal moraine, the presence of beavers and their dams maintains a wet and diverse valley bottom with areas of swiftly flowing water, recently ponded water, active dams, abandoned dams overgrown with willows, and old ponds gradually filling with sediment. As long as the beavers remain and the valley meets some minimum size that allows new trees to replace those gnawed down by the beavers, this configuration can persist for hundreds to thousands of years—a very stable state. But if something causes the beavers to leave the site, the wet meadow can transition to a dry elk grassland that is gradually invaded by upland vegetation, and this new stable state can also persist for a very long time. Some large input of energy or a dramatic change is required to cause the transition from one stable state to another, and returning to a previously existing stable state is not necessarily straightforward. This seems to be the case in Yellowstone, where some valley segments are returning to beaver meadows, but others are not.

Efforts to limit elk populations in Rocky Mountain National Park continue. Some of the former beaver meadows, such as Upper Beaver Meadows, have tall fences to exclude elk and deer. The difference between the groves of willow and aspen within the fenced area and the grasses and small shrubs outside the fence is striking. The fences are part of long-term riparian restoration being undertaken by the park service. The idea is to allow large enough riparian forests to grow back to support a beaver colony. Once the beavers are able to build dams and feed themselves, they will create beaver meadows that will be self-sustaining. This strategy will take decades to implement, but it should work if elk grazing in the meadows can be kept to a level that allows the willows, aspen, and beavers to survive.

I return past Bridal Veil Falls to the shrunken beaver meadow along Cow Creek. I imagine the day when Moraine Park and Upper Beaver Meadows will once again be places where only the determined bird watcher or fisherman ventures into a maze of sticky-bottomed ponds and small holes hidden among the tall sedges. In the shaded ground along the valley bottom of Cow Creek, the leaves of wintergreen promise that new growth is returning and the meadow will soon be vibrant with flowers and insects. I think about the choices we can make to renew the beaver meadow here and wonder if someday I'll hear the slap of a beaver tail on a pond at dusk along this creek. I hope so.

June
Loch Vale: Secrets within the Scenery

June is the month in the park when the snows come hurrying from the hills and the bridges often go, to borrow from Emily Dickinson. Logjams often go, too. As I climb to Loch Vale in the Glacier Creek watershed, I pause briefly where the trail comes down to the creek in the midst of a grove of aspens now newly covered in pale green leaves. Several years ago, there was a very large logjam here. I counted more than a hundred logs wedged against one another in a tight mass that created a step more than 10 feet tall along the stream. Water ponded above the logjam, which also caught many items accidentally dropped into the creek upstream. While marking the logs with numbered aluminum tags, I found four plastic water bottles, a metal canteen, a camera, a pair of sunglasses, and a first-aid kit, all the worse for wear. Now the logjam is gone, an absence that gives me pause every time I hike this trail. What had been an abrupt step in the channel is now a continuous riffle and the only signs of the jam are small shelves of sand, silt, and twigs along the margins of the stream in what used to be the backwater above the jam.

The signs of accelerating seasonal rhythms surround me. Each week new wildflowers come into bloom. Now I see wild strawberries and white violets beneath the aspens. The few bird calls of winter have expanded into a complicated medley of the songs of robins, warblers, tanagers, sparrows, chickadees, and thrushes. Hummingbirds descend swiftly to investigate my red shirt and I hear woodpeckers hammering at tree trunks along the side slopes. The sound made by hundreds of gallons of melted snow rushing down the steep creek is deafening at close range.

I pass Alberta Falls and the hikers stopped beside it for photos. The logjams catch water bottles and gadgets floating in the creek and the waterfalls and scenic views catch hikers bound for the lakes in the upper valley. The trail switchbacks around the falls and then levels out on a straight stretch that provides the first glimpse of the continental divide. Glacier Creek lies far below the trail here, beyond a steep talus slope. Looking for research areas nearly two decades ago, I climbed down the talus slope to investigate the creek and found an old beaver pond gradually filling with sand. Over the next decade I returned once a year to resurvey the wood in the creek and watch as the remnants of the beaver dam broke apart and then vanished completely. Sic transit gloria mundi, or almost. Some of the sand and silt ponded upstream from the beaver dam remains on the valley floor, fixed in place for the time being by aspens and river birch growing quickly in the black soil rich with decaying organic material. These are the fine soils that leave my cuticles stained black for more than a week after I work in them, no matter how thoroughly and frequently I wash my hands.

Footprints of the Glaciers

The climb up to Loch Vale is a hike in the wake of a glacier. From Bear Lake, the trail ascends past Alberta Falls to the Loch, Timberline Falls, Lake of Glass, and then Sky Pond. The valley I climb to reach the Loch forms a giant staircase with lakes on the step treads and steep sections of creek separating each lake. This configuration is common in the park: Frozen Lake, Black Lake, and Mills Lake along Glacier Gorge; the Gorge Lakes—Highest Lake, Azure Lake, Inkwell Lake, and Arrowhead Lake; Odessa and Fern Lakes along Fern Creek; Emerald, Dream, Haiyaha, Nymph, and Bear Lakes along Tyndall Gorge and Chaos Creek; or Bluebird and Ouzel Lakes along Ouzel Creek. Each of these lakes represents a place where a glacier eroded the valley bottom more intensely. In some valleys the uppermost lake occupies a cirque, the bowl-shaped depression where enough ice accumulated to create a glacier. Other lakes occupy a depression partway along the glacier's path. On a map, these glacial lakes resemble beads strung along the thread of the creek. I think of them as glacial footprints.

Glaciers stepped down these valleys at least three times between 2 million and 10,000 years ago. The youngest glaciers reached farthest down-valley about 18,000 years ago, but were in full retreat only 3,000 years later. How do we know this chronology? Mostly from radiocarbon dating. Glaciers occasionally reveal an "ice man" (such as the famed Ötzi found on a glacier between Austria and Italy and radiocarbon dated as being about 5,000 years old), but mostly the ice does not contain plant or animal tissue that can be radiocarbon dated. Every time a glacier retreats, however, life crowds in to the newly exposed terrain. Rivers of glacial meltwater deposit rock fragments pulverized by the glacier and plants gain a roothold. Ridges of sediment trap the melting ice to form wetlands that accumulate peat. Pollen grains blown in on the strong winds at the ice front settle in the ponds and wetlands. One way and another, dead plant parts accumulate, and the time of death of the plants is recorded in their ratios of radioactive ^{14}C to stable ^{12}C. Those radiocarbon ages constrain the timing of glacial retreat: we know the glacier had melted from this point by the time these plants lived here, and perhaps much earlier. If a thick layer of organic material accumulates before the glacier advances again, the ages of the uppermost organic sediment can record the last time before the site was again covered with ice. When scientists accumulate enough of these dates for a region, they have a reasonable idea of the timing of glacial advance and retreat.

Starting in the 1990s, geologists trying to understand the timing of glaciation acquired a new tool in the form of cosmogenic isotopes. The isotopic ratios of aluminum, chlorine, beryllium, and other elements in the uppermost inch or two of rock can be altered by exposure to solar radiation. Analogous to a photovoltaic cell storing energy during exposure to sunlight, isotopes accumulate in the uppermost surface of a rock in proportion to the length of time the rock is exposed to sunlight over thousands of years. Movement and the accompanying abrasion can remove the thin layer in which the isotopes have accumulated, or a forest fire that generates intense heat can cause the rock to spall and slough the outermost layer. But as long as the rock remains stable and in place, the signal of cosmogenic isotopes will accumulate. By using known rates of exposure to solar radiation based on latitude and the specific configuration of a site, scientists can measure the ratios of these cosmogenic isotopes and infer how long a time has passed since a glacier scraped away at this bedrock or dragged this boulder along. Using cosmogenic isotopes has dramatically expanded our ability to work out detailed, site-specific glacial chronologies, revealing nuances of timing previously unknown and allowing us to rigorously test mathematical models such as Milankovitch's prediction that variations in the relative orientation of Sun and Earth could cause continental-scale ice sheets to advance and retreat.

Viewed over a period of decades, ice is hurrying from these hills, too. The remnants of Taylor and Andrews Glaciers send water and sediment down into the Loch. I consider them glaciers in name only: small patches of ice, gray with sediment, now nearly completely melted. When, as an environmental scientist, I think of the music of the spheres, I am not thinking of classical metaphors of planetary movements. I am thinking of the movements of water among Earth's spheres: atmosphere of gases, dust, and water vapor; hydrosphere of water; geosphere of soil and rock; biosphere of organisms; cryosphere of ice. The music of the spheres is the cracking of ice in a glacier, the susurration of snow blowing among grass stems, the steady plopping of raindrops on a pond, and the murmur and roar of flow in a river. How will the music sound if the cryosphere disappears?

This is a bad time in which to be a glacier. High elevation valley glaciers and ice caps, and even polar ice sheets, are melting at accelerating rates, shedding water and sediment from every surface. Some of the retreating ice exposes ground not seen for 2 million years, *terra incognita* for contemporary species of plants and animals. At the national parks famous for their glaciers, I have watched the succession of ecosystems through time simply by traveling toward the retreating glacier front. In Alaska's Glacier Bay National Park or Montana's Glacier National Park, the mature conifer forest most distant from the ice becomes progressively younger forest as I approach the glacier, then stands of pioneering deciduous trees like aspen and birch, and finally only fast-growing grasses and lichens on the newly deposited sediment near the ice margin. These glacier fronts are places of accelerating rhythms. Glaciers melt faster as global climate continues to warm. As glaciers entering the ocean melt, larger chunks of ice break off more frequently, launching icebergs into a sea of blue that sculpts each berg into fanciful shapes. Floods of meltwater reconfigure the landscape beyond the ice front, where landslides of sediment formerly trapped behind glacial ice create echoes like thunder. All of these events quickly disperse large volumes of water and sediment across the landscape, and plants and animals claim the newly exposed surfaces as home.

Here in Rocky Mountain National Park, glaciers seem like something from another world on this day full of summer's abundance. Pines scent the air and aspen leaves shimmer in a light breeze. All the flowers of the understory are in bloom. As the trail descends back to the creek and beneath the shade of the forest, I watch a spruce grouse lead a brood of fluffy little chicks among the undergrowth. All about us, the forest hums and twitters with insects and songbirds.

Fifteen thousand years ago, the valley of Loch Vale would have looked very similar to the rapidly retreating ice fronts of Montana and Alaska. Now spruce and fir mostly cover the valley floor and reach up the side walls until the rocky slopes grow too precipitous and unstable. This is old-growth forest, with many trees more than 200 years old. That's an old forest by human standards, but it's not even the metaphorical blink of an eye in glacial time. The trees here never reach the girth and height of the fabled, cathedral-like old-growth of rain forests, but there are some impressively large conifers around the Loch compared to younger trees in the region.

By collecting hundreds of cores about the diameter of a drinking straw from trees throughout the southern half of Rocky Mountain National Park, and then counting the annual growth rings within each core, Jason Sibold of Colorado State University created a map of forest age within the park. The map reveals a mosaic of forest ages that record the most recent stand-killing disturbance. Most of these disturbances were wildfires, from the 2012 Fern Lake fire to large fires in the late 1800s. In some parts of the park, the forest has regenerated since timber harvest that occurred before national park designation in 1915.

The trail splits and I follow the fork that climbs to Loch Vale. My route now follows the creek more closely again and I stop to watch an ouzel fishing the river. Each time the bird dives into the water it immediately vanishes beneath the white froth of bubbles, then reappears suddenly a few moments later, like a magic act. I continue on, climbing the last steep section, to emerge at the outlet of the lake.

I gladly sit for a while on a knob of smoothly polished bedrock at the water's edge, admiring the stunning view. Snow remains abundant around the lake in June, creating striking contrasts against the dark green conifers, gray rock, and tea-colored lake water beneath the azure sky. The freshness of the glacial topography is apparent. The valley has the classic u-shape of broad base and steep sides associated with glacial erosion. Given sufficient time, plants growing along the upper valley walls and cycles of freezing and thawing will break apart the bedrock and send it cascading down in rock falls and debris flows. The walls will gradually become less steep. Some of the sediment will accumulate along the valley edges, creating a narrower bottom and more of a v-shaped valley cross section.

Fifteen thousand years since the last major valley glacier melted might seem to be enough time to accomplish these changes. In a wetter climate, it might be. The primary limitation to changing bedrock into sediment in Rocky Mountain National Park is the dryness. The chemical reactions that weaken and alter bedrock require water. Heat does not hurt, either. Not much happens chemically during the long winters at high elevation. Even physical processes such as freeze-thaw weathering cannot occur until the temperature goes above 32°F for some part of the day. Traces of the Pleistocene glaciers persist for a long time in the park, nowhere more evident than lakes such as Loch Vale.

Dammed Lakes

I follow the trail around the Loch and continue up past Timberline Falls to Lake of Glass and then Sky Pond, a route that lingering snowpacks do not always permit in June. From the upper basin, I perceive the lakes as small features tucked into a narrow valley at the base of massive, nearly vertical granitic walls. Here at timberline the slopes are nearly treeless, supporting only wind-blasted krummholz. Krummholz, a German term now widely used in English, literally means "crooked wood." Many of the tree species present in this dwarf forest are the same as those present at lower elevations, but the force of the wind braids the branches into complicated skeins and gives many of the trees a comb-over, with all of their branches growing in the down-wind direction.

I do not see pikas, but I hear them whistling and cheeping at me from their nooks among the rocks. A marmot is bolder, coming fairly close, jauntily swinging its reddish brown tail as it moves. I pause where a rock glacier comes into the valley, catching my breath as I appreciate the dramatic scenery, all rock and vertical lines.

When people of European descent settled in the region after 1859, they evaluated these lakes from a utilitarian perspective. Farmers attempting to grow crops suited to wetter climates in the semiarid grasslands at the base of the Front Range needed a great deal of supplemental water. Lakes and streams throughout the region were manipulated and modified to meet the need. Numerous water diversions were built in what is now the national park prior to the park's establishment. Some portions of the proposed park around Grand Lake were withdrawn by the Bureau of Reclamation at the time of park establishment in order to use these areas for future water diversions. Dams were built to increase the water level at Bluebird (1914–1923), Sandbeach, Pear, and Lawn (1903) Lakes, so that more water could be stored in these natural holding tanks.

The intent in building taller dams above the natural bedrock ledges or moraine dams at these lake outlets was to retain larger quantities of water during the snowmelt season and then release the water to downstream croplands gradually during the growing season. This remains the operating regime followed at artificial reservoirs outside the park boundaries. Essentially, the early summer snowmelt peak flow is reduced in favor of a more sustained, smaller peak flow throughout the summer and into early autumn. This does not cause as much environmental change as many other human manipulations of rivers, but changing the characteristics of each year's high flow does affect plants and animals living within and along the river.

Most river species, whether insects, fish, or riverside trees, time their life cycles around the flow of water. Subtle cues—a change in dissolved oxygen or temperature in the river water—trigger an urge to breed or to release pollen. The plants and animals take advantage of what the rising or falling waters of the river can bring, such as downstream transport of plant seeds, newly exposed shoreline habitat for germinating seedlings, or access to floodplain "nursery" habitat for juvenile fish. These adaptations have conferred a competitive advantage on individual species over time. When the patterns of flow in a river are abruptly changed, the landscape of competition shifts, too. Some species may no longer be able to reproduce as effectively, and their absence in turn affects other species. The life of the river corridor alters.

Natural processes cause shifts in the characteristics of rivers, too: the advance and subsequent retreat of valley glaciers caused enormous changes in downstream rivers and the plants and animals adapted or went extinct. But even the most swiftly advancing glacier moves more slowly than water engineering: the ice, after all, moves at a glacial pace. The slower rate of change provides more time for species to migrate to newer, greener pastures or to evolve adaptations to the new environment. We know little about the details of river ecosystems in the Colorado Rockies at the time that people began to alter those ecosystems by storing and diverting water. Now we can only infer what changes might have resulted from nineteenth-century water engineering by examining reference sites such as North St. Vrain Creek.

As conceptions of the primary purpose of a national park changed with time, the park service gradually acquired and removed most of the dams and diversions on high-elevation lakes within the national park. Or, in the case of Lawn Lake, the structure removed itself by failing abruptly and triggering a large flood downstream. Signs of the historical dams linger in "bathtub rings" around each lake where the vegetation has not yet recolonized the lake margins exposed as removal of the dam lowered the water level.

A Fish in Every Lake

I return down-valley to the Loch, where two cow elk accompanied by calves wade in the shallows at the edge of the lake. The leaps of feeding trout speckle the water around the elk. Most of the higher-elevation lakes in the national park historically had no fish. Tall waterfalls created barriers to upstream colonization by the dominant native fish: greenback cutthroat trout (*Oncorhynchus clarki stomias*) on the eastern side of the continental divide and Colorado River cutthroat trout (*Oncorhynchus clarki pleuriticus*) on the western side. These fish can withstand extremely low water temperatures and can work their way upstream past low waterfalls, but they are not salmon that can leap upward tens of feet from a pool in order to surmount the thundering drops of the Columbia River.

I find a spot away from the wading elk and sit beside the Loch to eat lunch. A short-tailed weasel in its chocolate-brown summer coat darts agilely among the rocks, sees me, and disappears quickly. Cutthroat trout moving among the boulders near shore are more placid, as though aware that I have no desire to catch them. I enjoy watching the fluid grace with which they move in the water, but a lake without fish is hardly a lifeless body of water. To an angler or a bear, a fish is a very desirable prey. To many other creatures, a fish is a fearsome predator. These other creatures thrive in the absence of fish. The food web of a typical lake starts with bits of dead plants brought into the lake by creeks or dropped from the surrounding forest, as well as bottom-dwelling algae along the shallow margins of the lake and floating algae known as phytoplankton present all across the lake. A host of microscopic animals eat the bits of dead plants and phytoplankton. Among the lake inhabitants are chironomids, a type of fly that spend their larval stage on the bottom of lakes and streams; rotifers, microscopic invertebrates named for a structure around the mouth that resembles a wheel; tiny, floating crustaceans named copepods and *Daphnia*; and floating zooplankton. The crystal-clear lake water turns out to be thick with tiny organisms going about their lives.

The existence of such organisms helps to keep the lake water crystal clear. All the invisible animals provide at least two important functions. They are a good food source for larger insects and crustaceans, as well as amphibians and fish. And by eating dead plants, dead bacteria, and algae, the invisible or nearly invisible animals clean the lake water.

In some fishless lakes, amphibians such as salamanders and frogs are also present. Studies in diverse mountain lakes of western North America indicate that the variety and abundance of species is greater in fishless lakes than in lakes with piscine predators. Tiger salamanders, boreal toads, western chorus frogs, and wood frogs are present in Rocky Mountain National Park, although little is known about them. Each is listed as a species of concern, meaning that it may be perilously close to vanishing from the park. Hazards that can kill amphibians in the park include climate change, deadly fungi, and introduced fish, but the relative threat posed by each of these remains unknown.

Farther down the shore, an angler flicks his line a few times and drops a fly onto the water. A lake without fish is a boring lake for those devoted to fishing. Tourists exploring the area prior to establishment of the national park wrote glowing accounts of the fishing along the streams. Camping in Estes Park in the early 1890s, J. S. Flory wrote "What piles of fish around that camp!" (quoted in Buchholtz, 1983, p. 85). Early photographs of hundreds of fish caught from individual large pools hint at the incredible abundance of the streams in the region. Market fishermen caught these fish for sale in Denver.

As might be expected, fish populations could not sustain this level of harvest. By the time the national park was established in 1915, the park service felt that extra measures were needed to ensure that no fisherman left unsatisfied. People began to stock fish in the region in 1886, but the activity reached its heyday between 1917 and 1941. Cooperating with nearby state fish hatcheries, national park rangers got involved as soon as the park was founded. In 1915, Arrowhead, Sprague, Lost, Crystal, Lawn, Ypsilon, Fern, Odessa, Two River, and Bear Lakes were stocked with more than 5,000 trout each. None of the trout were native species. Brook trout from the eastern United States, rainbow trout from the Pacific coast drainages of the western United States, and brown trout from Europe all went into the streams and lakes of Rocky Mountain National Park. During the 1920s and 1930s the list of stocked lakes expanded to include Dream, Glass, Chiquita, Haiyaha, Sheep, Black, Emerald, Cub, Doughnut, Inkwell, Spectacle, Blue,

Sky Pond, Frozen, Green, and Loomis. The Civilian Conservation Corps was particularly active during the 1930s. Historical photos show cheerful-looking young men packing metal canisters full of young fish up the trails. By the time most of the stocking ended in 1968, more than 20 million trout had been stocked in the park.

This was the heroic age of fish stocking across the United States. Leading fish biologists set out to remedy the deficiencies of nature, taking great pains to keep fish alive in buckets of cold water during transcontinental train journeys or horse-packing trips to high elevation lakes. No one had any regard for natural distributions. Carp were introduced from Asia to New York in 1831 and then aggressively promoted in public relations campaigns throughout the United States as a good food source. Native fish viewed as less desirable species were actively removed to make way for more fishable imports, as in the infamous example of the Green River, a major tributary of the Colorado River basin. Four hundred and forty-five miles of the Green River between Pinedale, Wyoming, and the Colorado-Utah state line were poisoned with rotenone in 1962 to remove the native fish prior to stocking the river with non-native trout. The Upper Colorado River Endangered Fish Recovery Program began in 1988 with the intent of restoring four of the native fish species decimated by the rotenone poisoning. Thus far, millions of dollars have been spent trying to remove the introduced species and restore the endemic native fish species, which are found nowhere else in the world.

Exotic species are no longer stocked in Rocky Mountain National Park, but they are in the park to stay. The native greenback cutthroat trout is now a federally listed endangered species that is found only in the uppermost portions of some streams, where a barrier such as a tall waterfall prevents upstream migration by brook and rainbow trout. Populations of brook and rainbow trout are well established in some lakes and stream segments above waterfalls, however, thanks to historical stocking. These populations remain in part because of pressure from anglers. The existence of angling in national parks where hunting is banned reflects a dichotomy in societal attitudes toward fish versus other wildlife.

Invisible Ecological Cascades

I stand up to stretch and the trout dart away into deeper water. The wind has picked up, ruffling the water surface and hiding the signs of feeding fish. Momentarily, the lake appears fishless. What difference does it make if fish are now present in historically fishless lakes, or if brook or rainbow trout inhabit a stream once populated only by cutthroat trout? Unlike the presence or absence of beavers along a stream, the presence or type of fish makes little difference in the scenery. But like the beavers, the fish are part of a complicated cascade of ecological consequences.

Most of the organisms that live in fishless lakes can provide a tasty meal for introduced trout. Comparisons of otherwise similar lakes with and without fish indicate that when the fish come in, all the large zooplankton species and many of the bottom-dwelling invertebrates vanish. Large crustaceans disappear from the plankton, leaving rotifers and some types of copepods. With only small grazers present, large species of floating algae flourish and the clarity of the lake water decreases.

Does it really matter if tiny, more or less invisible organisms living in the bed sediments of a lake are no longer present? Like many of the invisible ecosystem changes that our society so readily ignores, it does matter. Bottom-dwelling animals burrow into and churn sediments, aerating the deeper layers. This allows microbes to start recycling nitrogen, phosphorus, carbon, and trace elements within the sediments. Some of these recycled nutrients dissolve into the lake water, where they can be extracted and used by algae and by rooted aquatic plants that are in turn eaten by animals. Like the stone cast into a pond that sends ripples out across the still water, the introduction of fish into a lake ripples through the biological community of the lake, creating persistent changes and consequences that we still do not fully understand.

Substituting one species of trout for another can also alter lake and stream ecosystems in pervasive ways. Energy in the form of food flows in both directions between a stream and the adjacent forest. Trees drop leaves, needles, and twigs into the stream. Microbes and stream insects ingest this plant litter and extract nutrients. In the other direction, bottom-dwelling insects such as caddisflies and mayflies that live the larval portion of their life cycle within the stream emerge as winged adults and are then preyed on by spiders and birds dwelling in the forest. Where introduced brook trout replace native cutthroat trout, these exchanges between the forest and the stream are altered. Brook trout pick invertebrate prey directly from the streambed, whereas cutthroats mostly capture insects drifting on the water surface. By eating the bottom-dwelling grazing insects, brook trout cause an increase in streambed algae. Brook trout feeding can also reduce the number of adult insects emerging from the stream by more than half, which can in turn cause a decrease in the riverside spiders that eat emerging insects. Even people not fond of spiders can appreciate that spiders are good bird food and that many songbirds also depend on the emerging stream insects that feed spiders.

Humanity has a very long history of homogenizing the natural world to the extent possible. From the extreme case of Eugene Schiefflin, a nineteenth-century New York pharmaceutical manufacturer who loved Shakespeare and birds, and therefore thought it appropriate to introduce every bird mentioned in Shakespeare's writing into the New World (think European starlings), to the inadvertent introduction of stowaways from ships (rats, zebra mussels), nursery stock, food, or packing materials, we have spread microbes, plants, and animals around the planet at a dizzying rate. Some of these introductions are benign in the sense that the introduced species does not particularly thrive. Other introductions are ecologically virulent: the introduced species becomes invasive, heading out on its own for parts unknown, in the process competing with native species or altering their habitat. Ecologists have been metaphorically tearing their hair out for decades, trying to make the rest of us understand how introduced species and homogenization of natural environments and biotic communities destroys biodiversity. Biodiversity is amazing in its own right: who wouldn't want to see and to protect a bird like the ouzel that surfs between the depths and the surface of a numbingly cold mountain stream, or a tropical archer fish that shoots insects down from the air by squirting a jet of water at them, or bioluminescent worms that live in caves and glow pale white, and on and on? But biodiversity is also critical because it creates resilience. When a glacier advances, some plant and animal species will not be able to adapt or migrate and will go extinct. Others will survive. As we steadily reduce the number of species present on Earth, we reduce the collective ability of living organisms to withstand all the slings and arrows that outrageous fortune will send their way, from warming climates to river engineering.

There Is No Away

The wind picks up and small whitecaps appear on the lake. As summer develops in the park, winds and moisture come increasingly from the east. Warm, moist air flowing inland from the Gulf of Mexico across the Great Plains rises abruptly as it meets the Front Range. Air rising from the plains carries more than just water vapor. Atmospheric transport gives a new meaning to the old song title that "It's a Small World, After All." Dust stained rust-red with iron oxide travels from northern Africa and falls on England as blood rains. Some of the dust also crosses the Atlantic to fall on Caribbean coral reefs, adding nutrients to the coral ecosystem, but also carrying a type of fungus that can infect the corals. Dust from the Gobi Desert crosses the entire Pacific and penetrates as far eastward within North America as Denver, causing air quality to fall below federal standards. Closer to home, dust from the Great Basin and southwestern United States settles on the snowpack in the Rockies, causing the snow to melt more rapidly.

The concentration of people and domestic animals living at the eastern base of the Colorado Front Range creates one of the most important sources for atmospheric deposition of nitrogen in the national park. Over the past century, human activities have caused enormous increases in the amount of nitrogen entering rivers and emitted into the atmosphere. We spread nitrogen lavishly on our croplands and from there the nitrogen washes into rivers and the ocean. Nitrogen comes out of the tailpipes of our vehicles and the smokestacks of our factories. The cumulative effect is much greater environmental concentrations of nitrogen since 1950, both globally and in the area around Rocky Mountain National Park. By the start of the twenty-first century, the proportion of total nitrogen introduced to the atmosphere as a result of human activities exceeded that produced naturally.

Nitrogen is an essential element for all living organisms but, as with other nutrients, too much nitrogen can create problems. In most natural environments, the presence of relatively small amounts of nitrogen limits the abundance of organisms such as algae that can directly utilize it. But when nitrogen falls from the sky in sufficient quantities, the algae feast and algal populations boom. A wealth of algae is bad news for many aquatic environments, including rivers and lakes. The algae take up other nutrients needed by plants and animals. More importantly, when the algae die, they sink to the bottom of the water body and decompose in a process that extracts dissolved oxygen from the water. Depleted oxygen levels can kill fish and other aquatic life, creating a condition known as eutrophication.

Eutrophication is now widespread in estuaries and nearshore

The stunning beauty of Loch Vale gives no hint of the atmospheric deposition that has been progressively changing the biochemistry of the soils and lake water during the past few decades.

zones such as the Gulf of Mexico. Increased nitrogen deposition can also affect high-elevation lakes and alpine and subalpine plant communities. The lakes experience eutrophication as floating algae populations increase. Increasing nitrogen concentrations in the water of Loch Vale and other lakes in Rocky Mountain National Park, along with increased abundance and changes in species composition of the algae, indicate the start of eutrophication in these lakes.

Sediment settling on the bottom of each lake preserves a record of changes in lake chemistry through time. Scientists have obtained vertical cores of these sediments from lakes across the eastern and western sides of the park. Thunder Lake, Bluebird Lake, Black, Jewel, Mills, Lawn, Dream, Emerald, and Solitude: the mud hidden at the bottom of each of these lakes that constitute some of the most iconic scenery in the park reveals that current nitrogen concentrations in the lakes are unique in the 14,000 years of history recorded in the sediments. These are the secrets that lie within the scenery.

As I resume my hike, I feel the quickening pace of summer all around me. I think of the other, more subtle accelerating rhythms: glacial ice melting more rapidly; plants and animals colonizing the newly exposed earth; introduced fish eating their way into lakes and streams, driving changes among the other creatures inhabiting those waters; and nitrogen steadily building in the soils and lake waters, pushing the lake ecosystem toward eutrophication.

Perceptions and desires have changed through time. All of the dams have been removed from headwater lakes. Native fish are protected and exotic species are no longer stocked. A change in attitude by anglers and a concerted effort to remove exotic fish probably could decrease the influence of introduced fish on river and lake ecosystems in the park. Changes in resource use beyond the park boundaries could reduce atmospheric inputs of nitrogen to Loch Vale and other seemingly isolated, pristine lakes. Steadily increasing public awareness that people can change ecosystems in the park, for better as well as for worse, gives me hope.

July
Forest Canyon: Enduring Rhythms

July—the height of summer—and I am ready for adventure. Parking the car at the Alpine Visitor Center and setting off across the tundra toward Milner Pass, I think about why we always refer to the height of summer and the depths of winter. Summer is the annual high point in terms of plant and animal growth and is probably the emotionally easiest season for most people. I certainly feel at the height of summer as I stride through the rarefied atmosphere of 12,000 feet, despite an overnight pack weighing me down. I am out for adventure with my friend Sara Rathburn, an experienced backcountry hiker. Our objective is to descend the length of the Big Thompson River in Forest Canyon and map the logjams as we go.

On a map of Rocky Mountain National Park, Forest Canyon is an anomaly: unusually straight, with no lakes, no roads, not even foot trails. Forest Canyon is the heart of the national park backcountry, less than a mile from Trail Ridge Road in horizontal distance, but one of the least accessible portions of the park.

Natural rivers never follow completely straight paths. The Big Thompson River in Forest Canyon has plenty of small bends and irregularities when viewed at closer scale, but the canyon is markedly straight compared to every other stream course in the national park. The Big Thompson does not substantially deviate from a straight line until it reaches The Pool, where the Fern Lake Trail crosses the river and then parallels it down into Moraine Park.

The anomaly of a sustained straight line in any natural landscape typically indicates some underlying geologic structure such as a fault or a very large joint in the bedrock. Bedrock formed under pressure in Earth's interior expands and cracks along joints as tectonic uplift or removal of overlying mass brings the rock to the surface. These initially minute cracks gradually enlarge and become the zones of weakness where weathering and erosion most effectively attack the rock.

Variations in the spacing of joints cause most of the valleys in Rocky Mountain to alternate downstream between steep, narrow bedrock gorges and wider segments with lakes and meadows. Where the joints are closely spaced, the rock weathers and erodes more easily, creating wide valleys. Where the joints are widely spaced, the rock better resists the processes that would dismantle it, and streams have a tough time eroding anything wider than a gorge.

Joints can show up at the surface of a rock outcrop as the tiniest, barely visible cracks. Joints that have been weathered for a long time can also form wide fissures into which climbers wedge their bodies to scramble up sheer rock faces. Many of the iconic landscapes of the national park reflect the spacing of joints large and small: the spacing of the projecting ridges of bedrock along the cliffs above Loch Vale; the size of the boulders in the Boulder Field on the shoulder of Longs Peak; and the long, straight path of the upper Big Thompson River.

Despite its horizontal proximity to Trail Ridge, the ruggedness of the intervening terrain effectively isolates Forest Canyon from the road. Portions of the canyon bottom are visible from the Forest Canyon Overlook in the park, but the overlook is barely visible from within the canyon. Because there is no trail into the canyon, the park service must grant special permission for backcountry use. This is rare, because Forest Canyon would also be a difficult place from which to rescue someone. Even the fish may be challenged to get up there. I spent one lunch break at The Pool watching a trout repeatedly leap upward in a mighty thrust designed to surmount the bedrock ledge into The Pool at the downstream end of Forest Canyon, only to slam against the rock and slide back into the water below.

Forest Canyon begins innocently enough. From the Alpine Visitor Center, Sara and I follow a trail toward Milner Pass and

Poudre Lake. The trail contours along the tundra between the Gore Range Overlook and Milner Pass and the walking is easy. Then, at an unmarked spot, the ground gradually slopes down to the east to meet the small creek that is the official headwaters of the Big Thompson River. The slopes are steep but grassy, emerald green in July and highlighted with a palette of flower colors. All the varieties of paintbrush are here, blooming in shades from scarlet to magenta, pink, sulfur yellow, and white. Morning dew still lies thick on the meadows and we are quickly wet to the knees. Where the slopes grow gentler along the creek, the meadow is particularly wet and we choose our footing with care. Here, too, we pass low, grass-covered berms across the valley bottom, easy to miss if you are not looking for them: the dams of beavers no longer present in the valley. White marsh marigolds bloom near bluebells and deep-pink flowers of rose crown and Parry's primrose.

Spruce and fir scattered along the upper slopes start to close ranks as we follow the Big Thompson downstream. The narrow creek cut into the grassy banks of an abandoned beaver meadow is fed by dozens of small seeps and springs and unnamed little tributaries, growing progressively into a cobble-bed stream of cold, clear water. What began as a broad valley head funnels down to a narrow canyon not much wider than the channel, with forested slopes rising steeply on either side. The trees grow taller and shoulder down to the stream banks in dense stands of old-growth forest that likely dates to the 1600s and 1700s.

As the trees age and die, they fall over, but take a long time to rot. Sara is 1 inch over 6 feet tall and I am 5 feet 9 inches in height, and we adopt slightly different strategies for getting around some of the fallen trees. I sometimes hear a disgruntled exclamation behind me where Sara is unsuccessfully attempting to duck under the big leaning tree that I just crawled below. I get stuck climbing over obstacles that Sara's long legs easily clear. Most of the trees still have branches protruding from the trunk and these take their toll on our clothing and skin. One small twig even hooks my glasses off my face and flings them into the forest, making me certain the twig is inhabited by forest gremlins. The closest thing we see to gremlins are the tassel-eared Abert's squirrels scampering easily about on the fallen trees. We watch with envy where trees bridging the stream provide the squirrels with aerial highways above the chaotic tangle of wood on the ground.

A Tree Falls in the Forest

A tree that dies in the subalpine forest of Rocky Mountain National Park does not necessarily go anywhere very fast. The tree can stand for another 150 years or more, creating habitat for cavity-nesting birds such as mountain bluebirds, mountain chickadees, flickers, and woodpeckers. Once the tree falls, another 600 to 700 years may pass before the wood is completely decayed. During this stage, the fallen logs can form what my colleague Kate Dwire describes as bacon strips on the forest floor: a concentrated hunk of carbon, nitrogen, and other nutrients that feeds and shelters organisms from fungi and tree seedlings to termites, small mammals, and birds. A tree falling into a stream usually decays more rapidly because the wood is continually wetted and dried as flow in the stream rises and falls. Sand and cobbles moving down the stream abrade the wood and batter the log apart. But even logs in the stream can last many decades.

As the abundant fallen logs reduce our progress to a very slow walk, I remind myself of the importance of this downed wood. Every angler knows the fascination of logjams. The floating wood from which the current creates haphazard yet intricately interlocked jams forms a fish magnet. Mountain streams can be like a firehose in a gutter—a rush of water that carries everything before it. Any tree that falls into the stream, let alone any pinecone or leaf, is swept downstream so fast that all the little denizens of the stream—the bacteria, zooplankton, aquatic insects and crustaceans—are hard put to retrieve any nutrients from the organic material rushing by. An obstacle that creates an area of slower flow and a holding point for even a few hours gives the little organisms a chance to start ingesting what I call "forest dandruff" and to extract the carbon, nitrogen, phosphorus, and other nutrients and once more convert these nutrients into living tissue. A logjam that spans the channel, ponding water upstream and creating a pool of low velocity, is a preeminent holding point. Aquatic organisms flock to these logjams and pools for food and for the variety of habitats present.

I took photo 9 in the color insert in a pool upstream from a logjam. In the foreground, the streambed is a mixture of sand and fine gravel. In the middle ground, a large, flat boulder is exposed. Sunken logs rest against the rear boulder and the upstream edge of the logjam is visible at left. The logjam itself has numerous little crevices and protected areas in which smaller fish can hide. A trout is visible at the back in this view.

Some of the insects and microbes present in streams live on boulders, some like sand and gravel, others like wood—each group can find its preferred habitat in the backwater pooled by a logjam. Fish can find areas with overhead cover in which to shelter from predators and areas of lower velocity in which to rest and wait for food to drift down on the current. A logjam and the associated pool is a perfect hot spot—or, if you prefer, sweet spot—for life in the stream.

A logjam also supports the hidden community beneath a stream. The hyporheic zone (from the Greek *hypo* for under and *rheos* for flow) is the shadowy twin beneath each channel—the river seen through a glass, darkly. Water from the stream channel is forced into the subsurface at sites of downwelling, such as those upstream from a logjam, flows within the hyporheic zone for a greater or lesser distance, and then returns to the channel at sites of upwelling, such as the exit slope of a pool below the logjam. Sometimes the water takes a more circuitous path, following a buried layer of porous gravel and surfacing a mile away from the

Sara at the upstream end of the big logjam, which extended another 150 feet downstream along the Big Thompson River.

channel at the back edge of a broad floodplain. Whatever the length and duration of its subsurface journey, the water reenters the stream transformed. Microbes in the hyporheic zone remove nitrates dissolved in the water. Temperature fluctuations are damped by the time beneath the insulating sediment. Larval insects living in the spaces between cobbles ingest bits of fine organic matter. Water returns to the surface purified. The hyporheic zone of a river has been compared to a vertebrate liver because of these cleansing functions.

In a river turbid with suspended sediment, hyporheic return flow can be visible as a line of clear water joining the muddy surface flow. In the clear water of Forest Canyon, the hyporheic exchanges are largely invisible. Unable to perceive the hidden magic of downwelling and upwelling, Sara and I watch a harassed parent gathering food around the logjam for its noisy offspring. A juvenile ouzel follows an adult closely, screeching repeatedly for food. The juvenile is nearly the size of its parent, distinguishable only by its slightly more fluffy appearance, plump outline, and behavior. At least mama or papa has good fishing around the jam.

Logjams and beaver dams are two sides of the same coin: each creates a similar backwater that fosters habitat diversity and overbank flows, with the greatest effects along portions of the stream having a relatively wide valley bottom. The wide-girthed conifers of old-growth riverside forest produce the best logjams, and the shrubby willows and spindly aspens of wetter valleys produce the best beaver habitat. A wildfire or intense wind that opens up the canopy of spruce and fir can allow aspens to colonize a site and support a beaver colony, and an abandoned, drying beaver meadow can gradually transition to a mature conifer forest, but the most extensive and persistent beaver meadows form just upstream from glacial terminal moraines, and the largest and most closely spaced logjams seem to occur farther up the river networks. Forest Canyon has the requisite conditions for lots of jams: old-growth forest that periodically drops very large trees into the stream and an environment unaltered by humans. The canyon is thus an ideal spot to study logjams.

My colleague Jill Baron of the US Geological Survey had hiked Forest Canyon and told me of the many large logjams along the stream. By the time Sara and I get there, we see a lot of remnants of logjams along the stream banks, but the stream has largely been swept clean. Logjams come and go. I have meticulously tagged more than a hundred logs in a large, seemingly permanent jam, only to have the entire jam break up and vanish within a year.

Many of the logjams in the park form around a particularly large fallen tree that partially spans the channel and remains connected to the bank via the tree's upturned rootwad. These ramped pieces are more resistant to the force of the flowing water and act like a sort of tollgate, trapping smaller pieces of wood floating downstream. Where two or more ramped pieces fall into

1. *Ouzel Falls covered in the ice and snow of January.*

2. *View from the east down the Upper Colorado River valley. The Grand Ditch is the pale horizontal line at upper right. The conifer forest spreading into the meadows at the valley bottom at right marks a past debris flow.*

3. *Moraine Park in March, with scattered patches of snow across the dried grasses. Forest Canyon lies in the depression at the rear center in this view west toward the continental divide.*

4. A bull elk in breeding condition during autumn.

5. A ground view of a beaver dam and the narrow beaver meadow along Cow Creek prior to the flood of September 2013.

6. *The glacially stepped valley that holds Emerald, Nymph, and Bear Lakes, just to the north of Loch Vale.*

7.–8. *Wood ear seen from above and below.*

9. Underwater view of the backwater created by a logjam along Hunters Creek. Note the trout at the rear of the view. The large, dark mass to the right of the trout is a huge boulder over which the water is falling, entering the pool and creating the bubbles seen below the water surface.

10. White-tailed ptarmigan (Lagopus leucurus) blend in well with the mottled gray and tan rocks of the high center.

11. *Aspen along the trail to Loch Vale, September.*

12. *Along Tonahutu Creek, prior to the 2013 fire.*

13. Mills Lake in summer.

14. Emerald Lake, early morning, December.

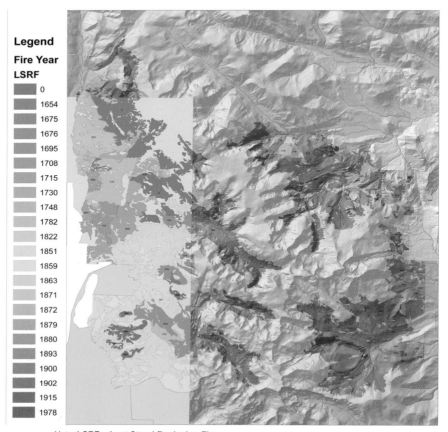

Legend
Fire Year
LSRF

- 0
- 1654
- 1675
- 1676
- 1695
- 1708
- 1715
- 1730
- 1748
- 1782
- 1822
- 1851
- 1859
- 1863
- 1871
- 1872
- 1879
- 1880
- 1893
- 1900
- 1902
- 1915
- 1978

Note: **LSRF = Last Stand Replacing Fire**

15. *A map of forest stand ages in the southeastern portion of Rocky Mountain National Park. The diagonal line near the top of the map is Forest Canyon. The fire years at the left side of the map, which reflect average stand ages for different portions of the forest, go from older than 1654 AD at the top of the scale to 1978 AD at the bottom. These dates indicate the diversity of forest ages throughout the area. Forest age across large areas of the map has not yet been studied. Courtesy of Jason Sibold, Colorado State University.*

the stream, the barrier can become nearly impassable to floating wood and every large piece of trunk and small branch coming downstream is trapped, creating a very effective low dam. But then something gives way: the dam is overtopped or undermined, a key piece rots and breaks, or portions of the upper dam are lifted and floated off by the rising water. Whatever the scenario, logjams in the park seldom last more than a few years. But new logjams continually form as the older ones are destroyed, and the number of logjams along a length of stream can remain relatively constant through time.

Forest Canyon is impoverished in jams when Sara and I explore it because of the extremely high flows that preceded our visit. The snowmelt peak of 2010 was unusually high and the peak of 2011 was high and unusually prolonged. Two successive years of anomalously high flows were too much for most of the logjams along the upper Big Thompson Canyon. I am surprised but not really disappointed. There is too much to marvel at within Forest Canyon to regret the jams that once were.

As Sara and I fight our way through the jumbled wood along the valley bottom, we are forced into shorter focal lengths. Because I am on my hands and knees and then crawling on my stomach with a full pack, I notice the sunlight shining through low-growing wood ear fungi, transforming the brown of the upper fungi into jack-o-lantern orange when seen from below. When I choose a tangle of undergrowth over a tangle of downed wood, I come upon the stunning scarlet berries of baneberry juxtaposed against the plant's deep green leaves. And, because I am effectively "nose to nose" with them, I admire the subtle creamy gold and reddish brown markings of a cluster of pinedrops, saprophyte plants that take their nutrients not from sunlight and photosynthesis, but from decaying logs.

These unlooked-for moments of delight are part of what makes the backcountry so special. I enter places where I see and hear no other humans, along rivers untrammeled by anglers and trails. I follow a stream that creates its own cool, moist environment.

Different plants grow in these valley-bottom microclimates than are present on the warmer, drier valley slopes only a short distance away. I see different animals—the beautiful pine martens that prefer slightly wetter forests in the park; sleek mink that move with equal ease on land and in the water; and tiny, round-bodied voles that fearlessly swim over vertical drops many times their height, seeming to surf the standing waves in the plunge pool below. These are places where every step must be considered and absent-mindedness is not appropriate.

When I hike an established trail, I find it too easy to slip into tunnel vision. I move swiftly and easily, thinking about other things because I do not have to devote much conscious effort to physically moving forward. I see a similar lack of attentiveness in other hikers. When my work along a creek brings me close to a trail, I am always amused that hikers on the trail seldom see me, no matter how brightly colored my clothing. When I am on a trail, the presence of other hikers distracts my thoughts. My mind goes skittering off into odds and ends and I have to work to stay focused on a research question or particular line of thought. Off trail, I give a great deal more attention and thought to my immediate surroundings. To take any footstep for granted or fail to look carefully is not only to potentially fall, but also to potentially miss an opportunity for the new insights that rise during these hikes like fish to a cast fly.

Fish are on my mind the evening Sara and I finally call a halt to our first day of hiking in Forest Canyon. Having seen remnants of logjams all day, we finally come to a huge, intact jam. The jam completely spans the channel in a wider portion of the valley, damming the flow so effectively that it creates a deep pool upstream and then spills over the banks and splits into multiple channels that meander across the valley floor before rejoining into a single stream a few hundred yards downstream. The pool is full of native greenback cutthroat trout. The fish are so unused to humans that they fail to startle and dart for cover as we move about the banks.

I sit and watch the fish moving with fluid grace between the light and shadows playing across the pool. This is what much of the park once looked like: deep pools full of fish and streams full of logjams. I study jams. I understand—intellectually—that any stream or river flowing through forest contained much more wood prior to the settlement of North America by people of European descent. Yet I still find it difficult to really conceive of just how much more wood there was. I read historical accounts of enormous logjams that stretched for many miles along the big rivers—the Red River of Louisiana, the Nooksack of Washington, the Maumee of Ohio, or the San Antonio River of the Texas Gulf Coast. I read of the hundreds of thousands of logs pulled from small creeks and big rivers as part of a national effort to limit overbank flooding, float cut timber to sawmills, and open navigational routes for boats. But I do not really assimilate this knowledge until I see the large logjams in remote streams flowing through old-growth forest in Rocky Mountain National Park: jams so closely spaced that long stretches of stream become a watery staircase of pools separated by a vertical drop over each jam. I try to imagine just how different the streams and rivers of North America looked and functioned before we got so busy "improving" everything. This is another part of the magic of discovering the hidden.

Leaky Rivers

The backcountry of the park gives me insights into how streams throughout forested regions of the world functioned before people cut riverside forests and removed wood from streams. The natural rhythms of tree growth and death, wood falling into streams, and logjams forming and breaking up endure in these most remote, least-managed portions of the national park. I find fascination and comfort in these enduring rhythms: the fascination of complex interactions among trees, streams, sediment, insects, and fish; and the comfort of natural rhythms across the seasons of a year and the years of decades and centuries.

The framers of the 1964 Wilderness Act envisioned wilderness, which they defined as a place where "the earth and its community of life are untrammeled by man, where man himself is a visitor who does not remain" as a place to rest and refresh the human spirit. As more and more people across the globe crowded into mechanized, polluted, highly engineered cities, the men writing the Wilderness Act legislation recognized the importance of quiet, uncrowded refuges for those seeking a change of pace. Wilderness provides such a refuge for me. Wilderness also provides a scientific benchmark, an environment in which I can study how streams function in the absence of human manipulation. At the start of the twenty-first century, only about 2 percent of river miles within the continental United States have not been directly altered by people—dammed, diverted, leveed, dredged, straightened, or riprapped—and many of those 2 percent are in Alaska. For scientists trying to understand stream form and function, streams that move to the rhythms of the natural world are rare and precious.

I can find these treasures in the backcountry of Rocky Mountain National Park, in streams that flow through old-growth forest and younger forest that has regrown after natural disturbances such as wildfire or blowdown. Comparing these streams to those in adjacent national forest lands with a history of timber harvest and floating of cut logs to sawmills, I find striking differences. My initial studies of the abundance and distribution of wood in streams throughout the park indicated substantial variations in stream configuration as a result of differences in valley shape and the age and history of trees growing along the stream. Wide, gentle valley segments with old-growth forest hold streams that repeatedly branch and rejoin around the obstacles created by closely spaced logjams. These are the streams where the flickering light on the pools alternately hides and reveals trout resting quietly in the shadow of a log, waiting for the mayflies rising and falling with the currents of warm and cool air just above the water's surface. I seldom actually see fish in the steep, narrow portions of the river where there are few logjams to retard the flow, and the water beats into a froth in tumbling down the steeply sloping bed of boulders. This does not mean the fish are not there, but I wanted to know how many fish occupy the steep sections compared to the gentle portions of the streams.

I put together a team of colleagues and graduate students to study the channel form and abundance of wood in the rivers, the numbers of aquatic invertebrates and their fish and riparian spider predators, and the metabolism of the stream. The latter phrase is one in which I take great pleasure. Metabolism is defined as the chemical processes that occur within a living organism in order to maintain life. Ecologists refer to the metabolism of a stream when they are studying how energy is created and used within an aquatic ecosystem. I like the phrase because it reflects the idea that a stream is analogous to a living organism: the stream creates energy through algal growth or the growth of nearby terrestrial plants that drop leaves and twigs into the stream, and the stream's use of energy is measured through the production of carbon dioxide, which reflects respiration by animals in the stream.

Our research team designed a study in which we made the same sets of measurements in streams flowing through both narrow, steep, and wide gentle valley segments with old-growth forest, younger forest with a history of only natural disturbances, and younger forest with a history of human disturbances such as logging. As expected, we found that the old-growth forests and wide valleys support the most physically complex streams. We also found that these streams hold tight to their nutrients. All of the logjams, side channels, hyporheic zones, and periodically flooded valley bottoms efficiently store carbon, nitrogen, and other elements vital to living organisms. We expected to find more macroinvertebrates—larval caddisflies, stoneflies, mayflies, and other aquatic insects—in these portions of the stream network. We did not, but that is primarily because the insects are so efficiently eaten: we found substantially higher abundance and diversity of fish and riparian spiders.

What is perhaps most interesting in our research is the pronounced difference between the natural and the human-altered sites. Even where the forest age and the valley form are the same, the streams with only natural disturbances have more—more wood, more physical complexity, more ability to retain nutrients, and more abundance and diversity of life. None of the human-altered sites that we studied has experienced timber harvest within the past half century. The differences that we measured are legacy effects from past timber harvest. When the trees are removed from an ecosystem, the ecosystem "remembers" for many decades.

I suspected that we would find many of these trends as we started the study, but much of my research lives and dies by statistics. One of the fundamental tenets of science is objectivity. An individual scientist may hypothesize based on observations that the world works in a certain way, but that hypothesis has to be tested by rigorously comparing it to large numbers of observations or experiments that can be repeated by other scientists. Statistics supply the toolbox that I use to evaluate whether my perceptions and hypotheses are likely to accurately represent reality. In the leaky rivers project, statistical analyses supported our original hypotheses, as well as revealing some unexpected patterns and insights, such as the difference between younger forests with natural versus human disturbances.

I use the phrase "leaky rivers" to describe rivers that have lost the physical complexity created by logjams, secondary channels, and hyporheic exchange. Lacking this complexity, the rivers are more likely to leak dissolved and particulate nutrients downstream, and are less able to support numerous and diverse plants and animals. By removing wood, channelizing rivers, and damming and diverting their flow, we simplify and homogenize them, so that the rivers leak. A few altered headwaters might seem like a dripping faucet: annoying, but not that much of a problem. But think of those calculations that water managers like to use to point out the cumulative waste of leaking faucets. One faucet with three drips per minute loses 104 gallons of water a year. In a river network, as much as 80 percent of the total length of river miles is typically in the small streams. If most of them become leaky, the dripping faucet analogy switches to something more like a gushing hose. We see the results of leaky rivers in the nutrient pollution that poisons so many estuaries and nearshore areas in the United States and other developed countries, exemplified by the "dead zone" that forms every year off the mouth of the Mississippi River. This area of nitrogen- and phosphorus-loaded water feeds enormous blooms of algae that consume the oxygen available in the water, killing or driving off other forms of life across an extent of ocean that can reach 5,800 square miles.

I remember this as Sara and I struggle through the lower third of Forest Canyon after the night beside the big pool. Unable to cross the swift river with our big packs, we work laboriously up and down the steep valley walls between bedrock cliffs and fallen trees that seem deliberately placed to impede us. We come to the biggest logjam I have ever seen in Rocky Mountain National Park, a dense tangle of hundreds of tree trunks protruding from the water as though they had been hurled like spears. The jam is a smaller version of the log rafts tens of miles long that once persisted for hundreds of years along the big forested rivers of the United States. Tired as I am, I smile, for I am seeing living history.

August
The High Center: Drama Visible and Invisible

The continental divide should be the great topographic crescendo of North America, a fateful point on the landscape that governs whether a falling raindrop travels to the Atlantic Ocean or the Pacific Ocean. Where the divide coincides with a narrow ridge of rock that drops precipitously on either side, the topographic drama lives up to expectations. In much of Rocky Mountain National Park, however, I look around and ask myself, where exactly is the divide? The divide meanders along the high center of the park, passing points where the drop-off is steep to both east and west, as expected, but for the most part obscure amidst the subtle topography. The high center of the park is not so much a concentration of towering peaks as a broad, gently undulating plateau at very high elevations, with individual peaks rising above the plateau.

The existence of the high center reflects hundreds of millions of years of geologic history. Each time the Rocky Mountains were uplifted, the topography was rejuvenated. Rock falls and landslides brought sediment from the hillslopes. Glaciers and rivers carried the sediment to lower elevations. As uplift slowed and erosion continued, the rivers deposited broad wedges of sediment from the mountains toward the east. Earlier iterations of the Rockies were much higher than today's mountain range and the rivers draining these heights spread sand and gravel worn from the mountains into the Great Plains as far as what is now the Colorado-Nebraska or Colorado-Kansas border. The central part of the mountains wore down to relatively round, gentle peaks.

As movement of molten material beneath Earth's crust caused renewed uplift, the relatively flat bedrock surfaces that had been created by prolonged weathering and erosion were lifted skyward. New glaciers and rivers cut into the flanks of the bedrock surfaces, carving deep valleys but leaving a central portion relatively unaffected—the high center.

Explaining why the continental divide in the Colorado Front Range includes some fairly flat but high-elevation landscapes leaves unanswered the question of why the Front Range, or the greater Rocky Mountains, of which the Front Range forms a part, even exist. That is a bigger geologic story.

The Mountain Rope of the Americas

The Rockies are a part of the Cordilleran Mountain system that dominates the western edge of North and South America. Cordillera comes from a Spanish word for chain of mountains, derived from an old Spanish phrase for rope. Depending on your linguistic background, you might pronounce it cord-ee-yera, or cord-i-lera. Either way, it represents one of the most impressive mountainous regions on the planet, extending nearly 11,000 miles from the Aleutian Islands to the tip of South America. The Cordillera is part of an even larger system of mountains that rings the Pacific plate, recording the tumultuous history of that portion of the planet, with segments in Antarctica, New Zealand, the western Pacific islands, and Siberia. The North American segment of the Cordillera is about 6,000 miles long, stretching inland almost 1,000 miles at its widest point at 40° N latitude, right in Rocky Mountain National Park.

Earth's crust deforms plastically as it sinks or rebounds beneath greater or lesser weight. The crust also behaves like a brittle solid, breaking and tearing under forces created by movements within the mantle. These forces have broken the crust into six major tectonic plates and multiple lesser plates. Over the course of geologic history the plates have been an unruly bunch, crashing into one another like bumper cars in a carnival ride, then pulling away again.

The continual shifting and jostling among the plates results in different types of plate boundaries. Where two plates come together in a convergent zone, the effects on each plate depend on their relative density. A dense oceanic plate converging on a lighter continental plate gets subducted, or forced downward into the mantle. This is an extremely messy, violent process. Any less dense portions of the subducting plate, such as volcanic mountains or islands, can be scraped off and accreted onto the edge of the continental plate. A geologic map of the western edge of North America is a colorful mosaic of different types and ages of rocks left behind by the Pacific plate as it descends into the depths. The edge of the Pacific plate does not go gentle into its goodnight: it sticks in place and then moves downward in an abrupt jerk that sends seismic waves out to shake the crust for hundreds of miles around. As heat and pressure increase with depth, the subducting plate begins to melt. Some of this less dense molten rock rises back toward the surface to break through in volcanoes or to bubble up the overlying rocks with magma that cools beneath the surface as a granitic pluton. The distance inland at which the volcanoes or plutons form traces the angle of the subducting plate. A steeply plunging plate produces mountains close to the coastline. A plate going down at a shallower angle deforms the overlying surface further inland.

The forces exerted on Earth's crust by the movements of tectonic plates through time hold the key to understanding the distribution and history of mountain ranges. All of the processes of mountain building are known as orogeny, from the Greek *oro* for mountain and *geny* for production. Most mountains are belts of deformed rocks that parallel the edges of continents because the mountains reflect the history of plate interactions along those edges. Deformed rocks can be folded where compressional forces cause the rock to bend, or faulted where compressional or tensional forces exert such abrupt stress that they break the rock. Rising magma can heat the overlying rocks, causing some minerals to melt and move in liquid form, and changing the composition and structure of other minerals in processes known as metamorphism (from the Latin *meta* for boundary or turning post and the Greek *morph* for form). Rising magma can also bow up the overlying rocks before cooling below the surface as an intrusive mass known as a pluton, from Pluto, Greek god of the underworld. Once the overlying rocks are removed by weathering and erosion, the pluton is known as a batholith if it is exposed over more than about 40 square miles. A batholith forms the core of many of the individual ranges within the Rockies, including the Front Range of Colorado.

It has taken a long time to create the complicated mountainous topography of western North America. The Cordillera reflects interactions between the Pacific tectonic plate and the Americas plate over an interval of nearly a billion years. These interactions continue today, as evidenced by volcanic eruptions and earthquakes along the west coast. Because the action has occurred along a predominantly north-south line, the Cordillera consists of mountain belts that also run predominantly north-south, with the Rockies occupying the interior belt of the Cordillera. The period between about 290 and 50 million years ago was a time of widespread mountain building throughout the Cordillera, and is sometimes known as the Cordilleran orogeny. The Cordilleran orogeny is given local names such as the Laramide orogeny, named after Wyoming's Laramie Range. The Laramide was a long interval of deformation that began 70 to 80 million years ago and ended sometime between 55 and 35 million years ago. During the Laramide, as during earlier orogenies, stress from the subducting Pacific plate deformed the western side of North America. Now I sit on the topographic remnants of that deformation, appreciating the clarity of the August sunlight and the broad sweep of space all around me.

High Summer in the High Center

The pace of geological change is currently slow in the high center, and the area appears deceptively benign on this sunny August morning. The heroic tundra flowers are in bloom, the size of each

*A yellow-bellied marmot (*Marmota flaviventris*) in the high center at the peak of summer.*

blossom dwarfing the rest of the diminutive plant. White-tailed ptarmigan hens lead groups of swiftly growing chicks in foraging among the dwarf willows. Pikas dash about among the boulders, uttering their sharp squeaks that can be so hard to trace back to the actual animal. Marmots move at a more sedate pace, revolving their tails like crank-handles as they walk.

Despite the steady activity of the animals surrounding me, I think of Whitman's line, "I loaf and invite my soul." The start of classes at the end of the month looms on the metaphoric horizon, but for now I simply enjoy the feeling of fieldwork gradually winding down before classes ramp up—a breathing space in the busy year. Not a hint of cloud appears in the blue sky and even the wind is loafing for the moment. The world spreads out vast as I look north toward the Mummy Range and the Medicine Bows, east toward the Great Plains and the intervening ridges silhouetted by morning sunlight, south toward Pikes Peak, and west toward an alternating pattern of mountains and high, broad basins.

Winter better represents the challenges that limit the survival of the plants and animals of the surrounding tundra. Tundra is present at the highest elevations because the heights are too cold, too dry, and too windy for trees. Grasses, sedges, lichens, mosses, clubmosses, and a few dwarf varieties of woody shrubs hug the ground, able to survive because of their adaptations to the desiccating winds, intense sunlight, and extreme cold. These plants limit their exposure by growing shorter, slenderer, less-branched stems and fewer and smaller leaves. They store more carbohydrates in their roots after the growing season ends, allowing each plant to get a jump on spring by starting its growth at colder temperatures, growing quickly, and flowering and setting fruit earlier than plants at lower elevations. Many of the plants are covered with hair that creates a layer of still air immediately next to their stomata, the minuscule openings through which the plant absorbs carbon dioxide and releases oxygen, losing some water in the process.

Some animals of the tundra adapt by migrating to lower elevations during winter, like the elk or bighorn sheep that graze the tundra plants during summer. Others hunt incessantly to keep their metabolism stoked against the cold, or hibernate during the coldest times. Marmots, in particular, can hibernate for eight months. Accumulated fat is their sole source of energy during this long period of torpor—marmots do not worry about obesity—and the temperature in a marmot's burrow strongly influences how much fat the animal burns during hibernation. Young marmots have a faster metabolism than adults, so many of the young hibernate with littermates and share body warmth. Even so, long, cold winters decrease survival.

Ptarmigan use a different strategy, relying on layers of fat like the marmots, but also thick feathers that cover even the bird's legs and feet. Ptarmigan can remain still for long periods of time to conserve energy, and they take advantage of the insulation of powdery snow by burrowing beneath the surface to escape the coldest temperatures and strongest winds. Every inhabitant of

Hamster-sized American pikas (Ochotona princeps) *are some of the liveliest inhabitants of the high center during summer, as the animals leave piles of "hay" out to dry in the sun. Beyond carefully stocking the larder, pikas' small bodies fully covered in dense fur from the soles of the feet to the ears help them to survive winter.*

the tundra needs some special physiology or behavior to survive winters where the temperature can reach –21°F and wind speeds can exceed 200 miles per hour.

Some animals survive the alpine winter by storing food. One of the most endearing sights on the summer tundra is a pika darting between sheltered crevices as it lays out tiny piles of hay in the sunshine baking the boulder fields. I find pikas adorable, but their incessant activity in August is in deadly earnest, for they do not hibernate and now is the crunch time for laying in the winter food stores that will keep them alive. Many of the calls and social behaviors that I watch with delight are actually the pikas defending their hard-earned hay piles, for which the little animals selectively harvest plants with the highest caloric, protein, lipid, and water content available.

Pikas are so well adapted to cold that they are considered early warning systems for detecting global warming in the western United States. Continued monitoring indicates that pikas are moving to higher elevations, where higher elevations exist, in an attempt to find suitable habitat and cooler temperatures: if they cannot find refuge from the heat, pikas can die in six hours when exposed to temperatures above 78°F. When you live near the top of a mountain to start with, however, it can be hard to find suitable habitat by going up in elevation. Recognition of this dilemma for the pikas, along with evidence of decreasing pika populations, led the National Park Service to start the Pikas in Peril Project in 2010. The project focuses on identifying at-risk populations and seeking solutions that may keep the pikas alive as temperatures continue to warm.

Imagining overheating pikas running out of cooler land to move up to is a grim thought and a reminder that heat can be as implacable as the tundra's winter cold. On a summer morning, however, the world of the tundra strikes me as gentle: the air is just pleasantly warm, the hiking easy, and the views stunning. Getting caught above timberline in an August thunderstorm can provide more insight into how much happens up here. Air masses heavy with water vapor sweep inland from the Gulf of Mexico, moving across the flat interior plains with little interruption. The enormous topographic obstacle of the Rockies forces the air masses to rise, causing the water vapor to cool, condense, and fall as precipitation. The foothills of the Rockies and the middle elevations, up to about Estes Park, receive the greatest volume of rain, as well as the largest amount of water per hour. By the time the air masses rise above the high center, much of the moisture has been wrung out of them. This can be hard to believe when getting drenched in an August thunderstorm, but the storm won't last long enough or drop enough rain to cause floods in even the small creeks present at the highest elevations. I had one memorable day of fieldwork in the high center that changed from a cloudless sky to what appeared to be the end of the world—black clouds and hail zinging in at a

45-degree angle—and then back to a cloudless sky, in just over an hour.

Blowing in the Wind

The winds coming from the east that drop nitrogen over Loch Vale, gradually acidifying the lake waters, also deposit nitrogen across the high center. Alpine soils and plants have limited ability to absorb and store nitrogen. The characteristics that allow a biological community to sequester this nutrient—thick, stable soils, abundant vegetation, a long growing season, and diverse communities of soil microbes—are absent in the alpine zone. Steep slopes, shallow, rocky soils, sparse vegetation, a short growing season, and low rates of uptake by microbes and plants all limit the ability of alpine biological communities to use nitrogen. When excess nitrogen falls from the sky as dust and with rain and snow, the excess shows up in the plants. The diversity of lichen species declines as some species die off in response to the extra nitrogen. Plant species able to take advantage of the bonanza, mainly grasses and some species of herbaceous flowering plants such as clovers, increase in number. This causes increased rates of nitrogen cycling in the soil. The effect is as though the ecosystem has been switched to high speed: nitrogen reaches saturation levels and then starts to leak everywhere—into water running off the surface and entering streams and into gases emitted from the soil during the growing season. Eventually, streams and lakes can become acidified.

Ecologists and biogeochemists study the high-elevation biological communities of the park, sleuthing out the clues that reveal subtle changes through time. These studies show that the continental divide separates more than the downward flow of rivers. The western side of the national park receives about 1 to 2 pounds of nitrogen per acre each year from atmospheric sources. The eastern side, which gets upslope winds coming off the urban areas, crop fields, and animal feedlots at the base of the mountains, receives about 3.5 to 7 pounds per acre each year. The "about" preceding these numbers reflects very local differences. Half of the annual nitrogen deposition in the park occurs during the nine months of winter, when snow blown across the landscape by strong winds accumulates in lee areas and then melts, releasing its load of nitrogen. As a result, some sites receive up to 9 pounds of nitrogen per acre. Not surprisingly, these sites show the greatest response to enhanced nitrogen. By 2003, long-term records of alpine plant species indicated significant changes in the abundance of individual species during the preceding twenty to fifty years. Seventy-five percent of the increased east-side soil nitrogen can be accounted for by increased nitrogen deposition associated with human settlement of the regions beyond the national park. The remainder appears to result from global increases in nitrogen released to the atmosphere by human activities.

Despite the lower population density of the western United States, the region is more urbanized than even the mid-Atlantic portion of the country. Eighty-six percent of people in the western United States live in cities and the entire region has experienced high population growth since the 1970s. Although the western part of the country as a whole has relatively low background rates of nitrogen deposition, areas downwind from cities, such as Rocky Mountain National Park during spring and summer, are hot spots of elevated nitrogen deposition.

Rocky Mountain National Park is not unique in this respect. A comprehensive survey of eight national parks in the western United States indicates that, despite our best intentions to set aside national park lands "to conserve the scenery and the natural and historic objects and wildlife therein, and . . . to leave them unimpaired for the enjoyment of future generations," as stated in the 1916 National Park Service Organic Act establishing the national park system, the parks exist within a greater landscape and air-scape beyond the control of the national park service. Air, vegetation, and snow at Glacier National Park contain high concentrations of pesticides coming from agricultural lands outside the park, as well as highly toxic synthetic compounds such as PCBs associated with an aluminum smelter. Air, vegetation, and snow in Olympic National Park contain mercury, PCBs, and pesticides. The story is repeated over and over, at Mount Rainier, Sequoia and Kings Canyon, North Cascades, Grand Teton, Crater Lake, Lassen Volcanic, Yosemite, Great Sand Dunes, Bandelier, and Big Bend National Parks. Even the far-flung reaches of the national park system are not so far for atmospheric transport: Wrangell–St. Elias, Glacier Bay, Katmai, Noatak, Gates of the Arctic, and Denali in Alaska contain historically used pesticides, mercury, and other contaminants, albeit at lower levels than national parks in the lower Forty-Eight. Every national park in the country in which scientists have assessed pollutants shows some level of contamination from sources outside the park boundaries.

The trends revealed by these studies suggest the importance of long-term monitoring and the importance of comparing diverse sites across the country. Acid rain received a great deal of attention starting in the 1970s because huge swaths of forest in regions downwind of industrial sources of sulfur and nitrogen began dying. The death of a forest is analogous to late-stage diagnosis of aggressive cancer: the problem has been developing for a long time and it is difficult to effectively halt the disease by the time it becomes obvious. In the case of forest die-off or lake eutrophication, the levels of acidity in the soil and water have increased over decades, triggering a cascade of changes in chemistry, microbial communities, and nutrient processing that cannot be quickly reversed. If long-term monitoring allows us to detect problems before they reach a crisis stage, there is hope that we can act to alleviate the situation causing the problem. Knowledge is only half the battle, however: knowledge has to lead to action.

Invisible Engineering

The high center epitomizes the invisible changes occurring within Rocky Mountain National Park. From the air come the nitrogen, mercury, pesticides, and PCBs that leave no obvious trace on the landscape but nonetheless insidiously work their way through the ecosystem, changing soil, water, and biological communities. And deep below lies the equally invisible engineering that sends water from the western side of the continental divide flowing to the east.

The national park map includes a dashed blue line, straight as a ruler, from Grand Lake on the west to a site labeled East Portal, just outside the park boundary on the east. This is the Alva B. Adams Tunnel, one component of the massive Colorado–Big Thompson Project that transfers water from west to east.

Water users have been eyeing Grand Lake as a source of water for the eastern slope for more than a century. An 1889 study evaluated the idea of cutting a canal across the mountains from the lake to South Boulder Creek. Proposals to divert Colorado River water directly through the Rockies via a tunnel date to a 1905 engineering class project at Colorado State College. The original proposal involved diverting water from Grand Lake to Moraine Park. The idea was revived in 1933, but met with strong objections from the park service. The park service worried about problems ranging from inadvertent draining of high-elevation lakes if the tunnel pierced fractures in the bedrock, to the unsightly disruption associated with reservoirs, power stations, and electrical lines. However, the politically powerful Bureau of Reclamation supported the project and state politicians and local newspapers aggressively promoted the idea.

The compromise solution was to build the diversion, but make it less visible. Instead of a surface ditch, the water went into an underground tunnel. The eastern portal of the tunnel was moved to a site just outside the park boundaries that is less visible than a portal at Moraine Park would have been. Grand Lake is a natural lake and the artificial reservoir of adjacent Shadow Mountain Lake was created in part to allow pumping from this water body so that the water level in Grand Lake could remain constant. Franklin Roosevelt approved the project in 1937 and the first water flowed eastward through the 13.1-mile-long tunnel in June 1947.

Now, when I climb the Flattop Mountain, North Inlet, or Tonahutu Creek Trails up to the high center, or stroll along one of the spur trails from Trail Ridge Road, I cannot see it, but some 3,000 feet below me is a tunnel just under 10 feet in diameter that sends up to 550 cubic feet per second of water under the continental divide.

Just as the continental divide is the starting point for the journey of a metaphorical drop of water flowing to the Atlantic or the Pacific, the invisible water engineering of the Adams Tunnel is the starting point for the changes in flow that have altered rivers across the western United States. On the eastern side, the more abundant water released from dams at a steady rate throughout the growing season has transformed the Platte River of the western prairie from a broad, shallow, braided channel to a narrow stream meandering through densely growing riparian forests. On the western side, the steady suck of the Colorado River's water into thousands of canals and pipes has shrunk the once-mighty river into a salty trickle that no longer reaches the ocean in most years. The Adams Tunnel is not the only water engineering in the Platte and Colorado River basins, but it exemplifies the utilitarian hubris of water use in the western United States by rearranging water right at the start of each watershed. This history of altering rivers to facilitate human water consumption, navigation, and flood control is part of the reason that various agencies in federal and state governments now spend a great deal of time and money trying to restore rivers in each watershed.

Acting on Knowledge

Humans are hardly absent from the high center. Trail Ridge Road is a high-use corridor, complete with exhaust fumes, noise, and thousands of hikers. The road dramatically increased access to the tundra and was a controversial alteration of the high center. The first, unpaved road was built during 1929 to 1932, a period of increased emphasis on automobile access to national park interiors that also saw construction of the Sylvan Pass road in Yellowstone, Going-to-the-Sun highway in Glacier, and the Wawona road and tunnel in Yosemite. When Trail Ridge fully opened in 1933, 83,000 autos entered Rocky Mountain National Park. By 1938, that number increased to 200,000 cars. Steadily increasing visitor numbers after World War II seriously strained national park facilities across the country, and in 1956 the National Park Service began a ten-year program known as Mission 66. Among the infrastructure improvements implemented during this program was the paving and widening of Trail Ridge Road. Critics charged that making travel in the national park more attractive and comfortable detracted from the area's naturalness, as well as luring more visitors (3 million people a year by 1978) into the high center. The critics were right, but the road is now a fait accompli around which the park service must design management to minimize direct human impacts to the tundra.

Numerous signs along Trail Ridge Road emphasize the fragility of the tundra, where thin soils exposed by trampling feet can erode readily in the wind, but plants grow back to cover the soil only very slowly. No one realized exactly how slowly until a woman named Beatrice Willard decided to systematically study the tundra. Willard received an undergraduate degree in biology from Stanford University in 1947. She dreamed of becoming a naturalist-interpreter for the National Park Service, but such a position was largely closed to women during the 1940s. But, where there's a will, there's a way. Bettie Willard moved to Colorado in 1957 to attend graduate school at the University of Colorado, just as the park service was getting ready to start Mission 66. She began working along Trail Ridge Road, which at that time had few formal parking areas or trails, allowing visitors to wander freely. Willard established permanently fenced sites in alpine areas near Forest Canyon Overlook and Rock Cut and monitored these plots annually for almost forty years. The resulting research constitutes one of the longest known records of alpine plant recovery and indicated that hundreds of years would likely be needed for full recovery of alpine areas trampled to bare soil by the feet of park visitors. Willard found that tundra sites trampled by people during the course of one year could recover nearly completely within four years, whereas areas trampled for decades would need a long, long time to once again accumulate the small mineral grains mixed with dead plant parts—soil—needed to support living plants. As Willard wrote in a 1971 paper, "The time-factor in tundra recovery is quite shocking." Working with park service staff, Willard helped to develop trails that would channel future visitors like water flowing in a river network, thus limiting the impact of human hikers.

Willard taught at the Colorado School of Mines for many years and became famous for "belly botany" field courses, during which she had students lie on their stomachs to observe the details of alpine plants. She also wrote several technical papers on her research in the park, one of which starts with a wonderful opening line: "No civilized society has learned how to add Man to the landscape without robbing subsequent generations of resources and opportunities that are vital to their well-being" (Willard and Marr, 1970, p. 257). By teaching generations of university students, as well as leaders in business, industry, and government during her time on the President's Council of Environmental Quality, Bettie Willard did as much as anyone could to add humans to the landscape without robbing subsequent generations. The woman who had a hard time finding a place with the National Park Service during the 1940s because of her gender was eventually presented with the Outstanding Environmental Leadership Award from the United Nations.

The presence of alpine vegetation in Rocky Mountain National Park may also be endangered by warming climate. *Tundra* derives from a Finnish word indicating a land with no trees, but the trees are waiting on the margins. Ecologists predict that every degree of increase in average air temperature will allow the tree line to encroach on the tundra by 250 feet. Only a few degrees warmer—easily within the range that climate scientists consider a real possibility—and the tundra will vanish. When I think of the pleasure I have experienced in watching pikas and marmots on the tundra, or in paddling among little chunks of glacial ice snapping and popping as they melt and release air bubbles in front of Greenland's tidewater glaciers, I paraphrase Aldo Leopold's famous phrase: I am glad that I shall never be young without frozen country to be young in.

Pondering the largely invisible changes far overhead and beneath my feet as I walk the tundra of the high center, I come back to the meaning of wilderness. What does wilderness mean in this paradox of an altered and managed ecosystem that is nonetheless largely set aside from the most obvious human alterations? Do the changes in alpine soils and vegetation caused by nitrogen deposition really matter? Probably. Time will tell, but then it may be too late on a timescale relevant to humans to reverse or mitigate those changes.

The complexities and uncertainties in ecosystem response to atmospheric deposition and to manipulation of water supplies make it difficult to predict these responses and to manage for them, but they also give us reason to hope. Ecosystems are resilient. Recent research indicates that urban streams preserve more ability to support aquatic life and to purify polluted water through natural processes than previously thought. Forest soils and vegetation can gradually recover if the acidity of precipitation is reduced. Reducing levels of phosphates in household detergents during the

1970s resulted in noticeable improvements in water quality across the country. My ruminations always return me to the thought that we can mitigate the damage we have done in the past, but only if we work at it: knowledge has to lead to action.

September
Lawn Lake and Fall River Valley: Flood Rhythms

By the end of the first week in September, summer is clearly over. In most years, the first hints of golden and orange appear among the vegetation. Individual branches or whole aspen trees start to turn yellow, as do the willows in the valley bottoms. The leaves of wild strawberries become scarlet and steel-blue berries cluster along the branches of the ground junipers. Where elk congregate, the bulls are stripping velvet from their antlers and regularly emitting the high-pitched squeals optimistically described as bugling. The days have become noticeably shorter and are likely to start with frost. On some mornings the rising sun reveals a dusting of new snow on the highest peaks. Normally, this is the time of year that nobody thinks about rivers in flood. The summer thunderstorms are largely over and snowmelt is a long way off.

I think mostly about floods as I start up the trail toward Lawn Lake. I have hiked this trail before to see the traces of a dam-burst flood that occurred in 1982 and the splendid scenery of this valley. Now I return to see the effects of the latest flood. The flood of September 2013 disrupted the normal seasonal rhythms of precipitation making its way into streams. The rhythm of floods in the national park can be a regular seasonal pulse that nourishes river ecosystems. Snowmelt floods flush silt and clay clogging the spawning gravels on riffles, erode the streambed and banks to make deeper pools, and carry down a new load of nutrients from the surrounding forest. Floods can also occur as an irregular beat that seems as dangerous as a heart arrhythmia but is just as important to rivers as the annual snowmelt floods. I sometimes think of rivers as the veins and arteries of a landscape, circulating water that sustains plants and animals by carrying water, sediment, and nutrients. The analogy is not perfect, but the atmosphere would be the heart, delivering the life-giving water that circulates down the rivers. I doubt, however, that many people who were in the park during the flood think of the rain that fell over a few days in September 2013 as life-giving.

I visit Lawn Lake and the Fall River valley a year after the big flood to take stock and to think about why some streams in Rocky Mountain National Park responded to the rain very differently than others. Much more erosion and deposition occurred along the Fall River than along other rivers in the park. This responsiveness to the flood reflects both the river's glacial history and the more recent history of water engineering.

The Legacy of Infrastructure

Like many valleys in the park, the Fall River and its tributary the Roaring River step down in alternating steep and gentle sections. The upper Roaring River starts at Lawn Lake and flows gently down a broad trough in which a Pleistocene glacier left huge masses of sediment. Just before entering the Fall River valley, the Roaring River cuts steeply through the lateral moraine left by a glacier along the Fall River. Here the Roaring River lives up to its name, crashing down whitewater cascades lined by tall banks of boulders mixed with sand. Entering the broad, gentle main valley, the water then winds down a meandering channel over fist-sized cobbles.

This is a lovely morning to be out, clear and calm, although the clouds start to roll in by mid-morning, hiding the top of Longs Peak within an hour. I labor up the switchbacks on the lateral moraine and then proceed more easily up the rest of the Roaring River valley. Masses of boulders lie piled along the channel. The newly deposited rocks are nearly white, not yet stained darker gray by lichens and weathering. I pass the remnants of the dam that failed in 1982 and reach the lakeshore.

A glacial moraine dams the water in Lawn Lake. Early settlers in the region built on this dam, adding a 26-foot-high earthen mound across the natural dam in order to store more water for irrigation.

An outlet pipe built into the dam was used to release water and regulate lake level. Built in 1903, the dam served its purpose for many years, despite the lake's subsequent inclusion in Rocky Mountain National Park. Things unraveled in 1982.

At 5:30 a.m. on the morning of July 15, 1982, the Lawn Lake Dam abruptly failed. Lead caulking around the connection between the outlet pipe and the gate valve had deteriorated, allowing water to leak from the pipe into the earthen dam. At first the water probably seeped through slowly, a diffuse wetting front that would deserve sinister music if watched as a movie. As more water leaked from the metal pipe, the force of the flowing water began to dislodge sediment and create a path that then concentrated additional water flowing with more force. The process, known as piping, creates subsurface conduits analogous to human-made pipes. When the pipe grew wider and enough sediment was eroded, the Lawn Lake Dam collapsed. The failure released 674 acre-feet of water into the Roaring River. An acre-foot is a volume of water well described by its name: the amount of water that equates to a 1-foot-depth across an entire acre—325,851 gallons. (A football field covers 1.32 acres.)

I pause for a while at the lake before continuing up the valley past Crystal Lake to the saddle between Hagues Peak and Fairchild Mountain. Once I am past Lawn Lake, the region appears more remote and natural, without the long swath of pale boulders along the river that the 1982 flood created and the 2013 flood renewed. The 1982 dam burst created a peak flow of 18,000 cubic feet per second along a river in which the normal snowmelt peak flow is about 200 cubic feet per second. The enormous pulse of water released by the dam ripped up the forested river banks and swept along house-sized boulders left by the Pleistocene glacier. Where the Roaring River is slightly less steep, the flood left sediment. Where the river course steepens, the flood scoured from 5 to 50 feet into the streambed and widened the channel by tens of feet.

Although plenty of glacial sediment remains in the valley today,

Views from 2008 at the alluvial fan, looking upstream (left) and from the side of the Fall River valley, looking down onto the fan (right; the Fall River flows from upper right to left). Although some plants had colonized the edges of the 1982 flood deposits, the center remained a mass of unvegetated boulders before the September 2013 flood.

the floodwater of 1982 effectively carried much of the sediment nearly 5 miles downstream to the junction with the Fall River, where the flood spread across the wider, flatter Fall River valley. When water loses momentum, it drops sediment. As the 1982 flood peak declined, the water dropped 364,600 cubic yards of sediment, creating the Lawn Lake alluvial fan. This fan was up to 44 feet thick and spread across more than 42 acres, a pile of sediment waiting for the next flood.

Although the 1982 flood lost momentum in the Fall River valley, the floodwaters kept going, filling the sinuous, cobble-bed Fall River with sand up to 6 feet deep. Two miles downstream from the alluvial fan, the flood overtopped Cascade Lake Dam, a 17-feet-

high concrete gravity dam built in 1908 to supply a pipeline and hydropower plant. The flood didn't just wash lightly over the top: 4 feet of water flowing over the dam crest caused this dam also to fail, releasing another huge pulse of water. A diagram of peak river flow with distance downstream shows the effect of this second dam failure. The floodwaters had started to spread out and slow down in the broad Fall River valley, but the failure of Cascade Lake Dam spiked the peak flow once more.

Peak flow again declined in the relatively broad, gentle valley over the next 6 miles between Cascade Lake Dam and Lake Estes. The openness of the valley upstream decreased some of the force with which the flood hit Estes Park, but it was still bad enough. Most people had plenty of warning and escaped the floodwaters, although three people along the flood route were killed. The town of Estes Park and other entities sustained $31 million in damages at a time when the population of the town was only 6,000 during the winter.

The 1982 flood was about fifteen times the size of the largest previously known flood. The flood was a catastrophe for people and their infrastructure, but once a dam bursts, there is no longer a flood risk and neither Lawn Lake nor Cascade Lake Dam was rebuilt after 1982. What did the flood do to the river?

Floods and Rivers

The surge of floodwater down the Fall River filled the channel with sand. A great deal more sand eroded from the Lawn Lake alluvial fan during the 1983 snowmelt season, creating sediment loads a thousand times greater than those present prior to the flood. Over the succeeding decade, all of this sand slowly moved downstream, until the river once more flowed clear through alternating pools and riffles over a cobble bed.

A dam-burst flood from a human-built dam can substantially alter a river ecosystem, but the river recovers. Rivers are resilient. They redistribute sediment mobilized during the flood. River organisms—bacteria, aquatic insects, fish, riverside plants— recolonize the disturbed zone, moving in from sites downstream or from adjacent, undisturbed rivers. The flood was a disaster for the city of Estes Park and for the people who died, but not for the river.

I think about floods and disasters as I survey the view from the saddle above the Roaring River valley. North-northwest lie the Comanche Peak Wilderness and the peaks of the Rawah Range, with the Zirkel Range just showing beyond. The tundra flowers are done blooming and the alpine zone is distinctly autumnal, with tints of golden, orange, and burgundy among the olive-green leaves. Pikas chirp anxiously from a lichen-covered mound of rock, and a marmot bulked up for winter trundles across a grassy patch. The long views from the saddle foster a sense of detachment from the busy activity below, where heavy machinery shifts masses of rocks and logs dislodged onto the Fall River Road during the September 2013 rainfall. I sit on a soft, grassy tussock admiring the views until the wind picks up and hurries the scattered thunderheads together, when I retreat back down the trail toward the cover provided by forest.

The region around Rocky Mountain National Park does not get much rainfall. On average, Estes Park gets about 14 inches of precipitation, nearly half of which falls during the summer. Communities at the base of the mountains receive only about 15 inches of precipitation. All of this changed spectacularly during the week between September 9 and 15, 2013. The base of the mountains received between 10 and 18 inches of rain. Different portions of Estes Park received 6 to 11 inches and much of the national park received 6 to 8 inches of rain. That was enough rain to cause widespread flooding in Estes Park and at lower elevations. The flooding within the national park, although interesting, mostly did not do much damage to infrastructure. The exceptions were the Roaring River/Fall River area and West Creek, at the northeastern end of the park. A wildfire covering more than 1,100 acres burned a portion of the West Creek drainage during the summer of 2010. The 1982 Lawn Lake flood left an abundance of unconsolidated sediment along the Roaring River. In each case, the earlier disturbance probably contributed to the outsized response of the stream to the September 2013 rains.

The September rains created anomalously widespread flooding in Colorado. From Estes Park east to the Colorado-Nebraska border, high flows inundated towns, ripped out roads, bridges, and pipelines, and spread everything from sand and gravel eroded from floodplains to toxic chemicals leached from oil and gas operations across a broad swath.

The news media described the flood as unprecedented, but very large floods commonly receive this designation. During the week of the flood, a persistent low-pressure zone over the southwestern United States brought moisture from the tropics north into Colorado. The configuration of the jet stream and the presence of a high-pressure zone southeast of Colorado blocked this moisture from moving beyond the Front Range. A similar atmospheric configuration in September 1938 also produced widespread, damaging floods, but the population of eastern Colorado was much lower at that time.

News coverage of the 2013 flood focused largely on the damage to people and infrastructure. As always seems to happen after a flood, people spoke of "cleaning up" the rivers. They wanted to get debris out of the channels and get the rivers back into the channels present before the flood. Each of these expressions—cleaning up rivers and getting the rivers back into their channels—makes me cringe. When the debris in question is pieces of houses, cars, pipelines, or bridges, I'm all for getting it out of the channels. When the debris refers to trees toppled from the banks or sediment carried from upstream, the issue is much less straightforward.

A rainfall or snowmelt flood benefits a river. The flood may leave what looks like a mess, but that mess creates diversity of habitats—newly eroded secondary channels or cutoff meanders in which standing water or very slow flow provides nursery habitat for young fish, new logjams from trees toppled into the channel that create the backwater pools sought by fish, new moist sandbanks in which freshly deposited seeds of cottonwood and river birch can germinate. Habitat diversity is the foundation for diversity of species and ages of individuals within a species and thus for river health. An unusually large flood, such as the September 2013 flood, creates a range of new habitats that subsequent, smaller snowmelt floods help to maintain.

A really big flood does not necessarily wipe out river plants and animals, either. Animals, in particular, can migrate up tributaries, seek out zones of slower flow within the main channel, or otherwise survive the high water, ready to recolonize the newly created habitat after the flood. At least, animals can do that if human infrastructure and river engineering do not isolate individual animal populations by creating barriers to their movements. One of the sad stories I heard about the 2013 flood was the fifty or more beavers found dead on lower North St. Vrain Creek, pinned against a metal grill designed to keep wood out of a large culvert.

On this September day, the rain never materializes and I am lucky to see several large bighorn sheep that look much more impressive in these surroundings than the radio-collared bighorns seen from the road in Big Thompson Canyon. I reach the last, steep descent into the Fall River valley and look down to where the 2013 flood destroyed portions of the road and interpretive trail on the alluvial fan.

In addition to cleaning up the rivers, the other phrase I heard frequently after the 2013 flood was the need to put the river back in its place. The phrase has so many undertones: from the darkest and most anthropomorphic interpretation of unruly rivers that refuse to acknowledge their subservience to us, to a simple desire to return the river corridor to exactly what it was before the flood so that infrastructure can be repaired and people can follow established patterns. The irony of the phrase is that the rivers that migrated across their historic floodplains were in their places during *and* after the 2013 flood: only our misunderstanding of river dynamics made us perceive them as out of place.

Each of the cities snuggled up against the foothills—Fort Collins, Loveland, Boulder, Lyons, and others—is built on the floodplain and alluvial fan created by a river over hundreds to thousands of years. A river flowing from a mountain canyon onto a flatter plain typically loses energy and deposits some of the sediment carried in the flow. Depositing sand and cobbles on a floodplain or a fan causes the ground surface to become slightly higher in that area. Sooner or later, a flood overtops the banks and the entire channel moves sideways to another area slightly lower in elevation. This process periodically recurs over long periods of time, but if a large flood has not occurred recently and at least some vegetation has grown across the former channel courses, the dynamic history of the floodplain or alluvial fan may not be obvious to someone on the ground. The old channels do stand out with even a cursory glance at an aerial photograph: commonly, the differences in soil across the floodplain or fan appear as differences in vegetation, even if the floodplain is now plowed over for crops. If the floodplain is covered by an urban area the old channels are much more difficult to discern, until a large flood reclaims the floodplain for the river.

The repeated sideways movements of a river across its floodplain create diverse habitats for aquatic and riparian plants and animals. Historically, rivers at the base of the mountains had meandering or braided main channels surrounded by secondary channels, floodplain wetlands, and patches of cottonwood forest. The river and the adjacent floodplain were closely linked by movements of water, sediment, and nutrients. Snowmelt or rainfall floods shifted the main channel from side to side of the valley bottom, inundated the floodplain, and deposited organic-rich sediment as the floodwaters gradually receded back to the main channel. Water soaking into the valley bottom resurfaced as springs and seeps well away from the main channel, and hyporheic exchange cleansed the water of dissolved nitrogen. The floodplains were undoubtedly messy with downed, dead wood, marshes, and beaver-dam ponds. I think of them as gloriously messy in exactly the same way that a tropical rainforest is messy with lianas, epiphytes, termite mounds, and downed wood. In each case, the messiness results from the continuing, irrepressible give-and-take among rocks and soil, weather, hillslopes and rivers, and plants and animals. Scientists and environmentalists have effectively increased understanding that it may be a jungle out there, but it's also an incredibly diverse ecosystem. I dream of an equal awareness of rivers as not just unruly pipes that convey water downstream, but as rich ecosystems entitled to occupy the spaces they have created through time.

Build It and Suffer the Consequences

One of the lessons I took from the 2013 flood was that of "build it and then you have to protect it." Floods are natural disturbances that maintain the health of river ecosystems, but the construction of campgrounds, pipelines, roads, and bridges along rivers means that these structures must be protected from floods or rebuilt after floods. This leads to a great deal of manipulation and alteration of the river environment, even in national parks. River engineering typically creates more uniform, homogenous channels and floodplains. This decreases habitat diversity and isolates individual segments of a river network by blocking access to adjacent floodplains or blocking animal migration with structures such as irrigation intakes or culverts. How many people think about the effect of a culvert when they drive across a river? I never did until I became involved in a project to design culverts that would maintain the ability of river animals to move up- and downstream. That seemingly innocuous corrugated metal pipe can concentrate flow sufficiently to prevent upstream movement by salamanders or can create a vertical drop at the downstream end that prevents upstream migration by small fish. Each poorly designed culvert chops off another length of stream from an array of animals that might otherwise occupy the stream. With enough road crossings, the stream can become a series of disconnected fragments incapable of supporting much aquatic life. One study of national forest lands in Oregon and Washington identified over 6,250 road-stream crossings on fish-bearing streams, which equates to about one crossing every 3.6 miles of stream. Fishery biologists considered 90 percent of the culvert crossings to be at least partial barriers to fish passage, so that culverts blocked access to about 15 percent of the potential fish habitat on national forest lands in the region. For native fish species already under stress from other factors such as introduced fish, excess sediment coming from logged hillslopes and unpaved roads, and warming water temperatures, loss of access to 15 percent of their historic habitat is a serious blow.

Just like land animals, fish and other aquatic wildlife need to move. Movement of aquatic animals upstream and downstream helps to maintain a balance between predators and prey and allows animals to move to new food sources and habitat. Animals dispersing to new areas maintain genetic diversity between populations and can supplement populations in which birth of new animals is not keeping pace with losses to predation. Room to move ensures that animals can come and go as habitat is created or lost by floods, drought, or other disturbances. On larger rivers, animals repeatedly move between the margins and the center of the channel to reach areas of shallow and deeper water, swift and slow velocity, or cooler and warmer water. In the small streams most likely to have culverts, cross-channel habitat diversity can be limited, making movements upstream and downstream especially important.

As I look down on the Fall River detouring across the valley around the alluvial fan, I think that the greatest favor any society can do for its rivers, and itself, is to stay out of their way. Floods are natural disasters only because people live and build within floodplains that are prone to periodic flooding. The underlying folly of this practice is not unique to Colorado. Graphs of flood damage through time in the United States and in the world, adjusted for inflation, shoot upward alarmingly despite the enormous amounts of money invested in flood protection in the form of levees, bank stabilization, and dams. The explanation is simple: no structure is completely flood-proof, but structures provide a false sense of security that encourages people to continue to live and build within floodplains.

The Big Thompson River downstream from Estes Park exemplifies the folly of thinking that rebuilding stronger and better within the flood zone will prevent future damages. During the night of July 31 to August 1, 1976, up to 12 inches of rain fell in the area between Estes Park and the town of Drake. The resulting flood killed 139 people and caused $35 million in damages. It was the flood of record, an unprecedented catastrophe, a 1-in-10,000-year event, a freak of nature. People got busy right after the flood, rebuilding the road and the many houses along the river. Persistence and determination in the face of adversity can be admirable traits in some contexts, but not in this one. Less than forty years later, a flood of similar magnitude happened again and people seemed to be thunderstruck and outraged that the road was largely destroyed and houses were smashed and carried away. George Santayana famously remarked that those who cannot remember the past are condemned to repeat it. The Lawn Lake alluvial fan and Fall River valley are a form of living history different than those present in other national park units such as Antietam Battlefield or the Hubbell Trading Post National Historic Site, but the historical lessons of past floods are no less relevant than those of battlefields and cultural monuments.

Part of the problem is our limited ability to estimate how frequently really large floods will occur. Scientists initially interpreted the 1976 Big Thompson flood as the largest flood to have occurred within the past 10,000 years based on sediments exposed at the small town of Waltonia. Waltonia sits on an alluvial fan formed where a tributary creek joins the Big Thompson River within the river's canyon. Entering from river right, the fan forms a sideways bulge of sediment that constricts the Big Thompson River channel. The energetic waters of the 1976 flood eroded this constriction, exposing 10,000-year-old charcoal buried in the fan. Geologists reasoned that, given the age of the organic remains, this was the only flood to have reached sufficient depth to erode that portion of the fan. Continued research over the next few years, however, indicated that the Waltonia alluvial fan is analogous to a conveyor belt of sediment moving very slowly down into the canyon. A big flood can erode the lower part of the fan, but the continued downslope movement of sediment will gradually rebuild the fan. The charcoal exposed by the 1976 flood might have been deposited on the very upstream-most portion of the fan and taken

10,000 years to work its way downslope before being exposed by flood erosion.

Scientists continued to develop other lines of evidence—from flood scars on very old trees growing along rivers in Front Range canyons to the ages obtained from wood buried in gravel bars during floods and then left undisturbed as the channel shifted to another part of the floodplain—to understand how frequently the largest floods return to the Front Range rivers. Gradually, the average time between occurrences of a 1976-magnitude flood declined from 10,000 years to a few hundred years, to less than a hundred years.

Room for Rivers

Thinking about the September 2013 flood in the context of history raises an interesting question. How relevant is the occurrence of past floods if climate is changing? Precipitation varies through time. By any measure—annual rainfall, rainfall within a particular month, maximum rainfall within a 24-hour period, and over any time span—years, decades, centuries—rainfall is more changeable than consistent.

Widespread acceptance among hydrologists of the idea that indirect flood records such as flood scars on trees or the age of exposed sediments can be used to estimate the frequency of floods has occurred only during the past twenty years. Without such geologic and botanical evidence, the only way to estimate flood frequency is to use measurements of floods from stream gages. The oldest stream gages in the United States date to the last decade of the nineteenth century, creating a relatively short record from which to extrapolate the frequency of a large flood that may occur only once every 100 or 150 years. Most stream gage records cover time spans much shorter than a century, yet a flood that recurs on average once every hundred years is the basis for regulatory zoning throughout the United States. Faced with this dilemma, hydrologists made the convenient assumption that floods are random in time and space. This allowed them to use floods during any interval of time—say, 1950 to 1970—and assume that the relationship between flood magnitude and frequency can be extrapolated to longer time periods.

This assumption, known as stationarity, was never anything more than a convenient fallacy. The more we learn about variations in stream flow through time, the clearer it becomes that stream flow is nonstationary. Fluctuations in the jet stream produce decades of enhanced flash floods across the continental United States and intervening decades of few flash floods. Extrapolate from a flood-rich decade and you get one estimate of the so-called 100-year flood. Extrapolate from a flood-poor decade and you get a very different estimate. In 2008 a group of hydrologists published a paper with the wonderful title "Stationarity is dead: whither water management?" in the prestigious journal *Science*. That was the death knell of the convenient fallacy, and engineers and flood planners have been scrambling to adjust ever since. Beyond the natural fluctuations in stream flow associated with weather and climate, we have variations associated with changes in land use (urbanization typically increases the flood resulting from a particular amount of rainfall because of the increase in paved area, loss of floodplains, and efficient routing of water through storm sewers), as well as global warming.

This makes it difficult to definitively determine whether the rainfall of September 2013 is a phenomenon of warming climate or would have occurred without human-induced atmospheric increases in greenhouse gases. However, atmospheric scientists agree that a warmer atmosphere holds more moisture, so warming climate likely contributed to the large amounts of rain that fell during the September flood and, more importantly, may result in more frequent large floods in future.

Warming climate and associated changes in floods is one more uncertainty adding to the challenge of managing natural environments in Rocky Mountain National Park. We are too far along the path of increasing atmospheric carbon dioxide levels to stop climate warming, but we can give rivers the room to move and adjust to changing levels of flooding. The European Union has adopted a river restoration program named Room for Rivers. A national park is the preeminent place to leave room for rivers, and I smile at the thought of what a good chant the phrase makes: What do we want? Room for rivers. When do we want it? Now.

I start hiking early in the morning, while the conifers on the slopes above the Green Mountain Trail on the western side of the park remain frosted white from a light snow overnight. Increasing daylight reveals a thicker coat of fresh snow on the highest peaks. Cold breezes hurry me along and there is a look of winter in the gray light smudged beneath the last remaining clouds over the peaks. Soon the sun shines brilliantly on golden aspens running like tongues of fire through the dark green conifers.

October can be a relatively benign month in the park, with clear, warm days between nights when the temperature drops below freezing. Other years, October is the start of winter and quickly moving snowstorms coat the park in white even while the aspens and willows are still dropping their golden leaves. As in the case of September and floods, October is typically *not* a month prone to wildfires. But human-caused fires have their own seasons and rhythms. Portions of the old-growth forest along the Big Thompson River in Forest Canyon were scorched by a fire started in October 2012 when an illegal campfire near Fern Lake went traveling across the landscape. I think of this as I reach the area known as Big Meadows more than a year after the Big Meadows fire. I vividly remember the start of that fire.

Working in the forest along Glacier Creek the day the fire started, I glanced up at the sky to check whether the summer afternoon thunderheads had begun to coalesce. What looked like a volcanic eruption in progress shocked me to a stop. A thick, dark gray column of smoke rose to the north, apparently just beyond the nearest ridge. The smoke churned like a pot of boiling water, its height and width increasing as I watched. I called to the students I was working with and we speculated about the location of the fire relative to the car and camping gear we had left at the Moraine Park campground that morning. By the time we returned to the campground late in the day, smoke drifting across the continental divide from Big Meadows had settled densely in Forest Canyon and Moraine Park. Our eyes burned and watered and we tried not to breathe too deeply.

Even though the Big Meadows fire has been long extinguished when I hike through the burn area in October, the scent of ash and charred wood lingers in the air. Skeletal trunks remain standing, their blackened surfaces marking my clothes or skin if I carelessly brush against them. Patches of pale, unburned wood glow against the black where foraging woodpeckers have removed the burnt layer. An understory of herbaceous plants sprang up during the past summer, but the ground remains open between the plant stems, with gravel-sized particles still exposed to raindrops and water sheeting down the slopes in the absence of the thick layer of fallen needles that carpets a living forest.

The Big Meadows fire started about 3:30 p.m. on June 6, 2013, with a lightning strike in a grassy area east of Big Meadows. Fires in the national park are not aggressively fought unless they threaten people or infrastructure inside or outside the park, but people in the Colorado Front Range were extremely fire-shy by the summer of 2013, having experienced damaging fires in 2010 and 2012. Firefighters needed more than a week to contain the Big Meadows fire, which burned a little over 650 acres along Tonahutu Creek around Granite Falls.

Even a naturally triggered wildfire typically prompts questions about how long it has been since a fire occurred in the area and how long it will be before the forest recovers. To ask about recovery after a fire is to implicitly regard the fire as an anomaly, a disturbance that ruins a forest and something from which the forest must recover. We could justifiably turn the question on its head and ask how long it will be before fire rejuvenates a forested landscape. The framing of the question reflects our expectations of what is healthy or normal, but the answer to either version of the question is not so easy to determine.

Using annual growth layers in trees to map the age of different patches of forest, ecologists can reconstruct the history of wildfires and the changes in a forest ecosystem following a fire. Before people of European descent settled in the region, ponderosa pine forests between about 6,000 and 7,700 feet in elevation—mostly at the eastern edge of Rocky Mountain National Park and below—burned in low-severity fires at intervals of five to thirty years. These fires mainly burned the ground cover and did not kill mature trees. Started by lightning, these fires were particularly common during dry summers and typically occurred several years after a wetter year that favored the growth of understory plants. Forests of ponderosa pine and Douglas-fir growing between about 8,000 and 9,000 feet in elevation experienced alternating low-severity ground fires and severe, stand-replacing fires at intervals of forty to a hundred years.

At elevations of about 9,300 to 11,000 feet, within the subalpine spruce, fir, and lodgepole pine that form the most common type of forest in the national park, infrequent, high-severity fires started by lightning could kill all of the canopy trees over hundreds to thousands of acres. These fires recurred at intervals greater than a hundred years and commonly at intervals greater than 400 years. As with the fires in lower-elevation forests, these intense fires were triggered by lightning during times of drought.

These return intervals for fires are average values. One of the hallmarks of a natural or unmanaged forest is the diversity of tree ages among different stands of trees. A map of forest stand age for the southeastern portion of the park is like a jigsaw puzzle, with stands of trees less than 100 years old bordering stands more than 400 years in age (see photo 15 in the color insert).

How long it takes a forest to recover following a stand-killing fire depends on how you define recovery. Like a person progressively aging and undergoing different stages of maturity, a forest continues to change through time. Forest ecologists commonly differentiate an early stage during the first 100 years after a fire, when pioneer species such as aspen or lodgepole pine can grow

quickly to maturity and create shade that allows seedlings of more
shade-tolerant species such as spruce and fir to germinate. The
early-stage forest typically has many closely spaced, rather spindly
trees: a dog-hair forest. As some of these trees die, the survivors
and the shade-tolerant species become more widely spaced and
larger in diameter. After 200 years, the forest takes on old-growth
characteristics of large, old trees, abundant standing dead trees
and fallen trees, and a complex vertical structure of the forest
canopy. Even an old-growth forest can continue to change over
the next 200 to 300 years, with progressively more downed wood
accumulating on the forest floor and progressively larger trees
forming the overstory. An intense fire can kill old-growth forest,
but this is not necessarily a bad thing if the fire burns only a portion
of a very extensive forest.

Fire Ecology

The valley bottom remains relatively wide and the gradient gentle
as I turn onto the Tonahutu Creek Trail and continue upstream to
Granite Falls. Beyond this the trail steepens as it climbs up toward
the alpine zone at Bighorn Flats. I have wandered across the flats
in July, admiring the tundra flowers as a large herd of cow and calf
elk continually emitted high-pitched cheeps and whistles that I am
reluctant to call bugling. But today, as the cold wind reminds me
of the coming winter, is not the day for high-elevation adventures.
I move beyond the 2013 burn zone into green forest. I understand
the importance of wildfires, but I cannot help preferring the sight
of green needles and the shelter they provide from the steadily
increasing wind.

As with floods, wildfires are natural disturbances that are
fundamental to maintaining a healthy forest ecosystem. Nutrients
in the ash return to the soil after a fire. Some species of plants
require fire to complete their life cycle and some animals rely on
these plants. In Rocky Mountain National Park, many lodgepole

pines have cones that remain sealed by resin until the heat of a fire melts the resin and releases the seeds. Lodgepole pines do not germinate and grow under the shade of a mature forest canopy, but a fire triggers a new generation of lodgepole seedlings. The seeds of plants as diverse as short-lived wildflowers and long-lived woody shrubs are able to survive the heat of a fire and germinate in large numbers after the fire. As time between fires increases, populations of these species decline and the reservoirs of their seeds stored in the forest soil become depleted. Fire resets the ecological clock of the forest, maintaining forest diversity.

Ponderosa and lodgepole pine forests, in particular, are adapted to fire, but in different ways. Fire kills mature lodgepoles, but also opens the forest canopy and allows the germination of new lodgepole seedlings. In the absence of fire, lodgepoles tend to die out and be gradually replaced by trees such as spruce and fir, which have seedlings that need shade to germinate. Mature ponderosa pines typically survive fires except for intense crown fires. The more frequent ground fires keep the forest floor between the widely spaced mature pines open and sunny, allowing the germination of new ponderosa seedlings.

In addition to benefiting some species of plants, fire creates opportunities for insect-eating birds. Some species forage during the fire on insects flushed by the smoke and heat. Woodpeckers feast on the insects in standing dead trees in the years following the fire. Standing dead trees also create habitat for cavity-nesting birds such as flammulated, northern pygmy, and boreal owls and downy and hairy woodpeckers.

For many years, I imagined woodpeckers as having almost supernatural hearing that allowed them to detect beetles burrowing under the bark of trees. Then one day I happened to be sitting next to a dead tree while doing research in an area blackened by fire the year before. Sunlight reflected from the glossy black surface of the trunk as though the tree was sculpted from obsidian. I heard a crunching noise and looked around for a bird scratching or pecking at the tree. Nothing. Puzzled, I walked around the tree and scanned the surroundings. When I sat down again and listened carefully, it occurred to me that perhaps I was hearing a beetle foraging underneath the charred layer of the tree trunk. A little energetic digging with a pocketknife revealed a small beetle burrowing within the charred wood. The outsized noise made by the little insect reminded me of a night in the desert, sleeping without a tent, when I woke abruptly and hurriedly turned on a flashlight, afraid that a desert bighorn sheep was about to step on my head. A very small toad in the act of crossing my ground tarp blinked confusedly in the blinding spotlight.

As I study the patches of green trees within the burned area of the Big Meadows fire, I am reminded that even large fires typically do not kill all of the forest in an area. A much more common scenario is that a fire will burn a portion of a contiguous forest. This creates opportunities for plants and animals that thrive in the newly exposed area, while other species of plants and animals that thrive in the closed canopy and shaded understory of old-growth forests continue to exist in adjacent, unburned stands.

The healthiest forests are those with the greatest diversity of conditions. These forests support a greater variety of plants and animals and appear to be more resilient to disturbances. An even-aged forest can be highly susceptible to any particular form of die-off, from a beetle outbreak to a blowdown or a wildfire. Just as human societies with people of all ages survived the flu epidemic of 1918 that preferentially killed people in their twenties and thirties, trees of varying ages and varying species differ in their ability to withstand fire, flood, drought, pestilence, and intense winds. A diverse forest is more likely to be only locally affected by whatever challenges are thrown at it.

To Burn or Not to Burn?

Flow in Tonahutu Creek is at its lowest ebb for the year. Patches of bulbous ice edge the water where the creek remains shaded throughout the day. The flowing water creates swiftly flickering patches of light and shadow beneath the ice. Tonahutu is named from an Arapaho word meaning meadow. Bands of Utes lived in what is now the national park, but in 1915 the Colorado Mountain Club convinced the US Geological Survey (which has long been the arbiter of names for natural features because of its role in making topographic maps for the country) to change many of the place names in the park to Arapaho words.

Native Americans in many parts of North America used fire extensively to manage vegetation, drive game animals during hunting, and signal other tribes. The forest cover in much of the continental United States reflected this human-dominated fire regime when Europeans first reached the continent. The Ute and Arapaho tribes using the lands in and around Rocky Mountain National Park at the time of European contact were the latest in a long succession of occupants dating back at least 12,000 years. Low stone walls above timberline in the park appear to have been used by prehistoric Native Americans during game drives. Ancient projectile points have also been found within the park. The projectile points are composed of rock quarried in Middle Park, a broad basin of slightly lower elevation to the west of the national park. Archeologists interpret this to mean that prehistoric occupants of the national park region moved into the area during warmer seasons and spent winters in slightly more hospitable areas. These prehistoric occupants and their historic Native American successors were nomadic hunter-gatherers. There is no evidence that they deliberately set fires within the subalpine or montane forests of the national park region.

The frequency and severity of fires initially increased with European settlement. After trappers removed most of the beavers during the first decades of the nineteenth century, settlement in the Colorado Front Range lagged until the discovery of gold near Denver in 1859. That discovery triggered a series of rushes for gold, silver, and other metals. The sites of mineral discoveries moved back and forth across the mountain range for the next five decades. When a mining strike occurred, several thousand people could rush to what had previously been a largely unoccupied site. These communities had an enormous appetite for wood, which was used in every facet of life—houses, heating, roads, mine construction, railroads, and fuel to power the stamp mills that processed the metals being mined. Deforestation was intense and widespread, assisted by fires started from sparks thrown by railroads, stamp mills, and campfires.

All this removal of trees caused hillslopes to unravel in debris flows, creating so much sedimentation downstream that the farming communities springing up simultaneously at the base of the mountains petitioned Congress to do something. Congress responded with the 1878 Free Timber Act, which made it illegal to harvest live, standing trees on the public domain for commercial purposes. Miners and loggers responded by deliberately setting fires that killed the trees, which could then be legally cut.

Although the region of the national park was largely spared from mining, timber harvest did occur in the park. A sawmill at Hidden Valley supplied lumber for the Stanley Hotel. There was a sawmill along Mill Creek, the Griffith sawmill near Bierstadt Lake, a sawmill at Glen Haven along the North Fork of the Big Thompson River, and two sawmills at Lulu City.

A narrow band of aspens growing up the north-facing slope above Mill Creek forms one of the most visible legacies of these activities. I first noticed the aspens one October, when their golden leaves glowed among the surrounding conifers. A stand of what appear to be individual aspen trees can actually be an enormous single organism connected belowground by roots. Aspens are among the first woody plants to colonize a site newly bared by an avalanche or a flood, yet large aspen colonies can be up to

80,000 years old. I particularly noticed the aspens above Mill Creek because they did not appear to be following the common pattern by growing along the line of a creek. An interpretive sign at the Mill Creek trailhead enlightened me: the aspens mark the location of a tie slide, where cut timbers were trundled down the slope to be collected for transport to a sawmill. Forest succession will eventually replace the aspens with conifers that blend into the surroundings, but for now the aspens form a visual legacy of timber harvest at Mill Creek.

Now there is great reluctance to cut trees in this region, unless the trees are first killed by a natural process such as insect infestation. The change in attitudes toward forests in the Colorado Front Range during the first part of the twentieth century reflects similar changes around the world: once the forests largely disappeared, people realized they had value beyond that of board feet of lumber. Protection started with fire suppression in 1920. By that time, rangers in the national park wanted to protect the scenery that was a key part of visitor experience. National forests outside the park boundaries also experienced rigid fire suppression as part of the new attitude toward protecting forests. Throughout the Front Range and other parts of the western United States, land managers followed the so-called 10 a.m. policy: all fires should be put out by 10 a.m. the morning after they were first spotted. This policy persisted into the late 1970s, long after ecological research had begun to demonstrate the critical importance of periodic fires in maintaining a healthy, diverse forest ecosystem.

Natural resource policy typically lags scientific understanding because policy also reflects societal perceptions. Viewing a charred, smoking, and apparently lifeless landscape after a fire does not readily lead to the understanding that fire is beneficial. And people who build houses in fire-prone areas want nothing to do with wildfires, whether they keep the forest healthy or not.

I turn back at the junction with the trail up to Haynach Lakes. The snow grizzling the conifers earlier in the morning has melted and the air is warm enough for me to start shedding layers of clothing, but these autumn days are short and I want to be back well before dusk. As I descend through the 2013 burn area, I think about how the park service and the public have become more accepting of wildfires.

The 1988 Yellowstone fires were a turning point in societal perception of wildfires in national parks. A series of fires that summer burned 1.2 million acres. The fires were initially portrayed in the news media as a disaster in one of the crown jewels of the national park system. The National Park Service and forest ecologists played a vital role in changing this perception by making the broader public aware of the beneficial aspects of fire. Visiting Yellowstone to watch ecological succession in action became popular in the years following the fire.

Natural resource managers gradually began to practice controlled burns during the 1980s. This involves deliberately setting fires that burn smaller areas with less intensity. These fires are intended to maintain forest health and diversity and to prevent the accumulation of dead plants that can fuel severe fires. Controlled burns remain controversial, however, not least because they can escape control.

Controlled burns, as well as mechanical thinning to reduce potential fuels for wildfire, are now part of the management policy for fires in Rocky Mountain National Park. Because 95 percent of the park is wilderness, however, fires are allowed to burn whenever practical. This can require active public relations as well as fire monitoring and containment, because people accustomed to the dry, windy summers of Colorado are justifiably concerned about the possibility of a fire abruptly "blowing up" beyond the ability of firefighters to contain it. Visitors to the park and residents in the region also dislike the reduced visibility and asthma-inducing smoke associated with fires.

The 1978 fire along Ouzel Creek illustrates one scenario of fires in the park. Triggered by lightning not long after the park service

Regrowth in the fire zone near Ouzel Creek, thirty years after the fire.

adopted a "let-burn" policy, the fire was monitored but largely left alone, burning over 1,050 acres, until it suddenly sped up and threatened houses outside the park boundaries. At that point, firefighters had to work aggressively to keep the fire within the park boundaries. The 2012 Fern Lake fire, in contrast, spread into the remote, steep terrain of Forest and Spruce Canyons. Partly because the fire did not threaten infrastructure and partly because the area was so difficult to work in, the park conducted a relatively low-level campaign against the fire for about two months until winter snows largely extinguished the flames.

The Future of Fire in Rocky Mountain National Park
Greater acceptance of wildfires in national parks notwithstanding, people in Colorado remain on edge at the possibility of fire, not least because of the unusually large number of standing dead trees

left in the wake of the mountain pine beetle. These beetles feed on ponderosa, lodgepole, and limber pine. The perception is that dead trees equal greater fire hazard, but the reality is not so simple. Trees harboring beetles take some time to die. During the first few weeks of beetle colonization, a fungus carried by the beetle blocks the transport of water and nutrients within the tree, resulting in death. During this phase the needles remain on the tree, but within a year the needles turn orange. This is when the forest is most vulnerable to crown fires, because each dead tree still contains dry, fine fuel in the form of small branches and needles within the canopy. Once the tree has completely died and the needles have fallen off, the dead trees create gaps in the canopy, which limits the intense crown fires that kill living trees and spread rapidly. Scientists have written for several years of how standing dead trees dampen fires, but it is a message that society as a whole is extremely reluctant to accept.

Having gone decades without much timber harvest, Colorado entered a frenzy of tree cutting as beetle-killed forests spread during the first decade of the twenty-first century. Tree cutting in the national park has largely been restricted to corridors of human use—roads, trails, and campgrounds where a falling tree might kill someone. These areas are sometimes known as "sacrifice zones" in which environmentally sound management is set aside in favor of recreation and human safety.

Systematic studies of fire trends across the western United States indicate that fires are becoming more common and widespread. One study found that increases in the number of large fires during 1984 to 2011 were particularly significant in southern and mountainous portions of the West. Another found that large fires became markedly more common in the mid-1980s, particularly in mid-elevation forests of the Northern Rockies, where increasing spring and summer temperatures and an earlier spring snowmelt are efficiently drying the forests. A comparison of temperature, precipitation, and total area burned in the western United States between 1916 and 2003 demonstrated that years with large fires correspond to times of low precipitation, high temperature, and severe drought.

These relationships seem like common sense, but it is sometimes important to rigorously and objectively test common sense, because perceptions can be in error. In this case, statistics support common sense. Climate models suggest that continuing changes in climate and increasing drought severity will facilitate larger and more frequent fires in future. Changes in fire and drought will in turn drive changes in tree ages and the species composition of the forest. My colleague Jason Sibold speculates that the higher-elevation forests of Rocky Mountain National Park will in future resemble the open ponderosa forests of southern Colorado and northern New Mexico.

The future of fire in Rocky Mountain National Park remains an open question. Winters are likely to continue to warm. Combined with decreasing snowpack, this will lead to drier soils and vegetation and increased potential for severe fires. As humans encroach on the park boundaries from all sides, there will be more pressure on the park service to suppress and contain fires both because of their potential to spread outside the park boundaries and because of the air pollution widespread fires produce.

Long Live Wet Meadows

As I come back into Big Meadows I inadvertently flush a herd of elk out of the trees and into the meadow. I feel the damp ground shake with the force of their hooves. The sounds of their movement among the grasses resemble a strong wind approaching through a forest. I think of the Utes and Arapahos who depended on elk such as these for meat and how the name of Tonahutu reflects the importance of the extensive meadows. A meadow represents a place where trees cannot grow, either because the soil is too wet or because fire has at least temporarily removed the trees. Despite the absence of contemporary beavers, Big Meadows remains a beaver meadow and marsh area that is too wet for trees. Although such areas can burn, they are less likely to do so than the adjacent upland forest.

Past generations of beavers in Big Meadows built dams that blocked flow and caused channels to branch across the broad valley bottom before rejoining downstream. From the air, the active and abandoned channels resemble the tracks left by skiers slaloming down a slope. The low-angle autumn sunlight highlights subtle differences in vegetation and topography along the complicated turns and loops left by Tonahutu Creek, as well as the straighter lines of elk and moose trails that cross the meadows.

River scientists sometimes use a "string of beads" approach to restoring and managing rivers. Beads are the portions of the river where restoration is more feasible—national wildlife refuges along the Mississippi River, for example, that preserve broader floodplains and provide an opportunity to manage floodplain wetlands. The string is the narrow, simpler portion of river between each bead, where dredging, levee construction, and agriculture or urbanization limit the ability to re-create natural river processes such as periodic flooding. Restoring the entire length of a river may be neither feasible nor necessary to restore river processes that maintain diverse plant and animal communities: some ecological form and function can be restored by focusing mostly on the beads.

Mountain streams are also beaded as a result of natural processes. The rivers of Rocky Mountain National Park are mostly composed of strings—the steep, narrow portions in which water, sediment, and nutrients move along at a brisk pace and the valley bottom is barely wider than the creek. Between these strings are the beads of wider, gentler valley segments in which logjams and beaver dams help to create and maintain a broader floodplain and secondary channels.

Beads, whether enamel, glass, or gems, are the main attraction on a beaded piece of jewelry or clothing. Beads are also the main attraction in a river network, creating abundant habitat

Moose graze in Big Meadows before the 2013 fire.

that supports diverse species of plants and animals, and storing
nutrients and water to create a productive environment that
fosters greater numbers of individual organisms. To completely
mix metaphors in a chapter focused on wildfire, river beads are
the biogeochemical and biodiversity hot spots within the greater
landscape.

I grew up near Cleveland, Ohio, where the parks ringing the
metropolitan area are known as the emerald necklace. The name
aptly describes beaver meadows, which appear as brighter, lighter
green beads on the river-strings of the Southern Rockies. Restoring
or maintaining these beads affects the greater landscape. The
riverine beads buffer the uplands and other portions of the river
network against the extremes and create environments where
unique communities of water-loving plants and animals thrive
in the dry climate of the Southern Rockies. In particular, the wet
meadows maintained by beavers help to buffer the larger landscape

from the effects of fires, creating natural fire breaks that also help to maintain forest diversity. Beaver meadows also buffer rivers against floods, and the meadows can buffer rivers against droughts, as water stored in the subsurface helps to maintain surface flow when winter snows and summer rains fail. As I hike back down through Big Meadows, I think about how we will need these meadows— and the beavers that maintain them—more than ever in a warmer, drier future.

I've always enjoyed the line from Louisa May Alcott's novel *Little Women* about November: "'November is the most disagreeable month in the whole year,' said Margaret, standing at the window one dull afternoon . . . 'That's the reason I was born in it,' observed Jo pensively." I, too, was born in November and I identified with Jo. Now, far away from the Ohio childhood in which I read *Little Women*, I am leaning into a disagreeable November headwind as I climb the Glacier Gorge trail. The weather has been mixed over the past weeks: days of warm sunshine alternating with early winter snowstorms. Now the trail is clear but muddy in places and already packed into mounded ice where the path remains shaded at this time of year. A strong gust momentarily staggers me and I hear the weird creaking of the surrounding trees, a sound like a wounded animal moaning. This is the season for blowdowns and I glance warily upward at the trees swaying along the trail.

Winds of Change

I first heard stories of a great blowdown in Glacier Gorge in early 2012. An online search revealed photographs and posts by hikers, pinpointing the event to November 21, 2011. That day fell within a windy week during a month in which sixteen days had wind gusts exceeding 50 miles per hour in the subalpine forests at Loch Vale.

Windy winter days in the park can be both exhilarating and frightening. The wind creates a sense of urgency, of things on the move. If I'm lucky enough to have it at my back, I move along quickly on snowshoes or Nordic skis. If the wind is strong enough to start the trees swaying and creaking, the exhilaration takes on an undertone of menace, particularly where beetle infestations have left numerous standing dead trees.

The park is always windy, but from October to March it is more so. Average daily maximum wind speed in the subalpine forest can be nearly 50 miles per hour, even close to the ground, with gusts of up to 90 miles an hour. The jet stream of consistently eastward-flowing air over North America is referred to as a stream because it represents a concentrated flow, like a stream channel. And, like a water stream, the jet stream alternates through time between straight, meandering, and even braided. Sometimes the full force of the jet stream blasts over Colorado. At other times, the jet breaks up into branches and one of these passes across the state. Although extending high up into the atmosphere, the topography down where we live affects the surface expression of the jet stream. The Rockies are so windy because rapidly descending jet stream air cascades over the crests of the individual ranges in patterns that reflect details of the local topography.

Trees are remarkably strong. An enormous weight of snow can settle on them in a few hours during an intense storm and they can bend without breaking in a strong wind. In the spirit of scientific inquiry, while seeking to understand how debris carried on floodwaters can scar tree trunks, I have taken the largest branch that I can lift and swung it against a tree trunk as hard as I could. My exertions leave not a mark on the trunk of a mature tree. But even the strongest trees can snap or topple in exceptional winds. Trees can be severely damaged when wind speeds exceed about 60 miles an hour, but it is the gusts—which can be up to two times the hourly average wind speed—that do the most damage. Steep terrain of the kind present in Glacier Gorge can funnel and accelerate the wind, creating speed and the turbulence expressed in gusts.

The sound and the fury of trees being broken and toppled must be amazing. Visiting sites where trees more than a foot in diameter have been sheared off by wind, I think of the battles fought with cannons on wooden sailing ships. One of the greatest dangers during these battles was flying splinters, although splinter seems too dainty a word for shredded wood pieces several inches across

Mature tree snapped by high winds during a blowdown near Loch Vale.

and more than a foot long being hurled through the air by the force of a cannonball smashing into a ship's wooden hull. I can readily understand how such a piece of wood could wound or kill sailors, having come upon jagged splinters up to four feet long and a foot across that were shot dozens of feet through the forest when a tree snapped during a wind storm.

More commonly, the entire tree is uprooted and toppled, ripping up a wide slab of soil as it goes over. The size and shape of the tree and its roots, the strength of the tree trunk, and the depth and moisture of the soil all influence whether a tree breaks or topples. The shallow-rooted spruce, fir, and pines common in the subalpine forests of Rocky Mountain National Park are particularly prone to uprooting, and the resulting blowdowns are relatively common across the Southern Rockies. I realized how common once I started noticing areas in the park with large numbers of downed trees. Valley forests along Glacier Creek, Icy Brook, the North Fork Big Thompson River, North St. Vrain Creek, and Hunters Creek all had blowdowns during the winter of 2011–2012. Hidden Valley, Mill Creek, Bighorn Creek, the Big Thompson River, and the aptly named Wind River are among the areas in the national park with large blowdowns during the past few decades. Most portions of the subalpine forest in the park experience some level of blowdown every ten to twenty years.

This might seem as if blowdowns would prevent forests from ever reaching the august status of old growth, but blowdowns are typically small in size. Like a wildfire that burns one patch of forest and then leaps across a valley, leaving unburned forest between charred stands of trees, wind gusts can topple one tree or a few trees in a grove, while leaving neighboring trees untouched.

I started searching out blowdowns to investigate how they influence the logjams I had been studying for a few years before the 2011 blowdown along Glacier Creek. Trees that pull up a root mass and topple across a creek form an effective barrier to small pieces of wood floating down the creek, not least because most of the

A tree toppled during the blowdown along Glacier Creek pulled up a wide, flat slab of soil with its roots. The straight line at the base of the root slab is a metal tape 3 feet long.

branches of the fallen tree remain intact as it falls. If the first year's snowmelt after a blowdown is large enough to carry much wood down the stream channels, at least some of the smaller wood pieces will lodge against the downed trees that bridge or partially span the channel. The accumulation of wood helps to trap other wood moving down the channel and soon the smaller pieces of wood are tightly packed into a jam that ponds water upstream and creates a small waterfall on the downstream side of the tree. If the jam ponds enough water during snowmelt peak flow to send the water spilling over the stream banks, a smaller side channel can form. Flow in the new channel can erode the banks and topple more trees, creating additional logjams. Given enough time, the valley bottom can become a maze of smaller channels that branch and rejoin around logjams. These portions of the valley are hot spots that trap bits of leaves and twigs in pools and eddies. Microbes, bacteria, and stream insects feed on the plant detritus. Trout, ouzels, riparian spiders, and songbirds all feed on the stream insects. Wetland plants not found elsewhere along the stream flourish in the wet soils. All this starts from a violent wind that blows down the big trees.

By the time I first visited the blowdown along Glacier Creek, in July 2012, the park service had cut dozens of trees that had fallen across the trail, creating a clear path through the chaos. As part of my research, however, I left the trail to crawl and climb over, under, around, and through the tangled mess of downed trees. Well before the end of the day, I developed my own Dr. Seuss–like chant: One bruise, two bruise, red bruise, blue bruise. The exercise left me deeply appreciative of trails.

At first, I thought the area looked like someone had lobbed hand grenades into the forest, leaving toppled and broken trees strewn randomly. Then I gradually perceived a pattern as I hiked the perimeter of the blowdown area and climbed the valley wall to the uppermost extent of damaged trees. The swath cleared through the forest by the wind came down the east side of the Glacier Creek valley, leaving trees snapped 5 to 20 feet above the ground. Then the wind turned down the valley floor, uprooting many of the trees but toppling them in different directions. The pattern likely reflected a microburst, a type of downburst in which cold air accelerates downward, forming an extremely powerful downdraft that spreads out when it hits the ground surface.

As with blowdowns documented in other regions by forest ecologists, the intense winds that sheared off mature trees did not flatten everything in their path. Undamaged trees remained standing amidst the piled trunks of their former neighbors. One standing tree had even caught the upper portion of the adjacent tree when the latter sheared off. The number of standing, unaffected trees increased gradually toward the perimeter of the central area of greatest damage, but I also found little pockets farther away where six or seven trees had been toppled while the surrounding forest remained undamaged.

The size and intensity of blowdowns vary widely. In October 1997, winds estimated at 120 to 150 miles an hour in the Routt National Forest just northwest of Rocky Mountain National Park destroyed trees over nearly 25,000 acres. The affected area consisted of hundreds of smaller blowdown patches averaging about 60 acres in size, separated by equal-sized patches of undisturbed trees. The blowdowns occurring in Rocky Mountain National Park during the winter of 2011–2012 also mostly consisted of relatively small patches of uprooted trees among undisturbed forest.

Blowdowns leave a messy-looking forest, but they likely contribute to forest health by helping to maintain diversity of tree age and vegetation species present within the forest, just as fires do. Subalpine forests are particularly susceptible to blowdowns because of more shallowly rooted trees, shallow or poorly drained soils, and more frequent extreme winds than lower elevation montane forests. Stand-killing forest fires occur only infrequently in the subalpine zone. This makes blowdowns even more important as a local disturbance that kills some trees, but also opens new sites for herbaceous plants and other tree species, such as aspen or lodgepole pine, to germinate.

The Beetles Are Coming!

Blowdowns are not the only natural disturbance shaping the subalpine forests. Part of the challenge in understanding how these forests change through time is the synergy among blowdowns, beetle kill, and wildfire, particularly as climate warms in the next few decades. The integrated picture that emerges from individual scientific studies is a sort of perfect storm descending on subalpine forests in the national park under a warming climate: Warmer winter temperatures help mountain pine beetles and promote a longer wildfire season. Fire-injured trees can be more susceptible to beetles and to blowdown. Blowdowns can trigger beetle outbreaks. Blowdown-affected stands can burn more severely. All signs point to likely increases in the frequency, extent, and severity of disturbances to subalpine forests. This in turn points to smaller areas of old-growth forests in future.

The most visually apparent sign of forest die-off in the national park and surrounding national forests at present is the trees killed during the past decade by mountain pine beetles. When I started my logjam surveys on the eastern side of Rocky Mountain National Park, I felt a sense of urgency. I had watched broad extents of forest on the western side of the continental divide change from green to orange within a few years and I knew that I had a relatively brief window of time to document patterns of instream wood before the pine beetles reached the east-side forests and started to change patterns of tree mortality and wood recruitment to rivers. So I worked day after strenuous day one summer, egging myself on during periods of fatigue with a chant running through my head: The beetles are coming! The beetles are coming!

The mountain pine beetle is a native species that creates at least localized forest die-off every few decades. The current beetle infestation in western North America may be the largest and most intense that has occurred within the past few hundred years, although some ecologists dispute this. Whether unprecedented or just unusually extensive, the current beetle epidemic has killed millions of trees and altered forested landscapes in ways that many people find unsettling.

Considering just the numbers, it's impressive that any stand of forest can reach old-growth status. Bark beetles as a group range from northern Canada to northern Mexico and from sea level to 11,000 feet in elevation. Seventeen different species of bark beetles live within Rocky Mountain National Park. Different species of beetles feast on lodgepole pine, ponderosa pine, limber pine, Engelmann spruce, subalpine fir, and Colorado blue spruce, which together constitute a large proportion of the conifer species in the region.

There may not be a single "smoking gun" explanation for the current extensive outbreak around the national park, but the relatively even-aged forest that has regrown largely in the absence of fires after widespread deforestation in the late nineteenth century is commonly assumed to be part of the explanation.

Progressively warming climate likely also plays a role in the current beetle success (to consider the infestation from a beetle-centric viewpoint). Longer summers equate to more beetle reproduction—perhaps twice as much. Biologists Jeff Mitton and Scott Ferrenberg discovered that mountain pine beetles are now reproducing twice each year instead of once, resulting in exponential increases in beetle numbers. Working at a field site at 10,000 feet elevation with a long-term temperature record, Mitton and Ferrenberg noted that air temperatures have increased over the last forty years. The pine beetles have responded by metaphorically getting a jump on spring. The beetles start their flight season more than a month earlier than indicated by historical records and they just keep going, flying twice as long as in the past.

Adult beetles emerging from trees in late spring search for a living tree that they attack en masse. The beetles start to excavate egg galleries within a day and lay eggs within a few days. Speeded along by warm temperatures, the eggs develop more quickly during the summer, resulting in adults that emerge in August. It is this summer generation that has not previously been present in beetle populations. All those beetles need room to grow, so the species has also expanded geographically, killing trees 450 miles farther north in Canada and 2,000 feet higher in the Rocky Mountains than reported from previous beetle outbreaks.

Low winter temperatures (around −40°F for more than a week) can kill beetle eggs and larvae wintering under a tree's outer bark and thus limit beetle survival, but such prolonged cold snaps are becoming uncommon. The warmer winters and drought-stressed trees present in the Front Range during the past two decades probably favor widespread beetle infestation.

Confronted by a massive die-off of trees, park service officials face some unenviable decisions. On the one hand, they are supposed to minimize interference with natural processes. On the other hand, no one wants to have visitors killed by falling trees. Trees in high-use areas including road corridors, campgrounds, parking lots, and visitor centers can be selectively or completely removed, as in the case of the Timber Creek campground on the western side of the park, which I now call Timberless Creek. Trees that the park service describes as high-value trees important for shade, visual screening, and esthetics are being sprayed with the insecticide carbaryl, which must be applied directly to the trunk of every single tree each year until the beetle outbreak eventually subsides. As park service literature demurely puts it, "there are adverse impacts with chemical spraying," so carbaryl is not a viable option for preserving wide swaths of forest.

If trees could shiver with fear, they should be doing so now. One study published in 2009 has already documented a rapid increase in tree mortality rates within unmanaged old-growth forests in the western United States during the past fifty years. The rate at which individual trees die (rather than mass die-offs in fires or blowdowns) has been doubling at intervals of seventeen to twenty-nine years across varying elevations, tree sizes, tree ages, and tree species. Even the young trees are dying faster than they used to. The scientists who conducted the study attributed these changes to climate warming and increased water stress in trees.

Other plants will grow where these trees die. Spruce and fir species of subalpine forests might be replaced by pine species now characteristic of drier and more open montane forests. At lower elevations, montane ponderosa pines might be replaced by the pinyon pines and junipers now growing in the chaparral zone, or by dry grasslands. These are the types of changes that have occurred during the past 10,000 years after the Pleistocene glaciers retreated.

Individual plant and animal species altered their geographic distribution as the warm, drier period of 7,000 to 5,000 years ago, for example, gave way to much colder temperatures about 4,000 years ago. In each period of change, individual plants and animals do not just pack up and move. A great many individuals die and some species go extinct. With luck and room to move, some of their offspring colonize newly suitable habitat. The difference in this particular period of climate change is that human alterations have severely restricted the ability of many species to disperse to new habitats. Cities, roads, dams and reservoirs, or farm fields: for some species of plants and animals, these constitute impassable barriers. The other difference in this period of climate change is that humans are present to witness and understand the causes and consequences of the change.

Living Downwind

Hiking up to the old-growth forest along Glacier Creek on this windy November day, I reach the outlet of Mills Lake only by leaning so far forward into the wind that I am mostly looking at my feet. Even though the morning is well advanced, much of the lake remains shadowed by the low-angle sunlight and the surrounding bedrock walls. A snowshoe hare and I regard each other for a long moment. The hare, which in summer turns brown but for its hind feet, has now transitioned back to a coat of winter white. Another blast of cold wind makes my eyes water. The hare turns back into the protection of the forest.

I lean into the wind, thinking about the rigors and dramas of winter. Metaphors of sleep and death aside, a lot happens in the national park during the winter. Avalanches roar down steep slopes. Glaciers grow—or at least, they used to. Patches of forest topple and snap in blowdowns. And the wind brings in not only snow, but also dust. More and more dust, recently.

Aeolus was the god of the winds in classical mythology, and

scientists refer to wind-blown dust as aeolian inputs. Mostly this dust is silt and clay particles less than a tiny fraction of an inch in diameter, but the composition of these particles varies widely. Some of the dust particles are the nitrates and mercury that I described in connection with Loch Vale and the park's high center. Other particles are calcium picked up by the wind from eroding soils or phosphorus and carbon derived from bits of dead plants blown in on the wind. Dust has been blowing into Rocky Mountain National Park for millennia, adding important minerals to the soils. We know this because the dust shows up in sediments accumulating in lake beds, meadows, and streams across the park. The dust also collects in glacier ice and in each year's snowpack. Vertical cores through the sediment and ice reveal that dust inputs vary through time. Dust deposition increased between 1850 and 1900, for example, and then declined for a while. The decades of increased dust correspond to the period when people aggressively disrupted native vegetation across the region, harvesting timber in the mountains and plowing the shortgrass prairie into croplands.

Dust deposited across broad sections of the American West has increased substantially during the past twenty years. This is clearly visible in Arizona, where the frequent occurrence of giant dust storms known as haboobs makes the news. The increased dustiness is also visible in the dirty snowpack that now characterizes the Rocky Mountains each year. Unless fresh snow has just fallen, the snowpack can be so dirty that it appears distinctly tan or gray even from the elevation of a commercial flight over the mountains.

A more precise indicator of the increased dust inputs comes from the National Atmospheric Deposition Program (NADP), which has monitored calcium and other dust inputs at numerous locations across the United States since the 1970s. At monitoring sites on the western slope of the Rocky Mountains, calcium deposition has increased by 400 to 500 percent during the past twenty years as dust storms from Arizona, New Mexico, and Utah increasingly blow across the region. Some of this dust from the southwestern United States does not make it over the continental divide, but enough does to show up at NADP sites on the eastern side of Rocky Mountain National Park.

I huddle into a sheltered spot among the trees at the edge of Mills Lake, enjoying the wintry look of my favorite lake in the park. High bedrock ridges south of the lake block much of the low-angle sunlight of November and the lake remains shaded for much of the day, creating a scene composed in shades of gray and white. No one else is here today and the lake feels isolated and pristine. I get the same feeling at Loch Vale, which lies just across the ridge crest to the northwest. The pristine look is deceptive, however.

Loch Vale is one of the NADP sites. My visits there make me appreciate the heroism and dedication of the scientists who actually conduct the NADP sampling. The phrase above that describes the NADP sounds innocuous: "monitored calcium and other dust inputs . . . since the 1970s." What this means in practice is a trip into what is commonly a remote site, strenuously difficult to access, every Tuesday. No matter what Tuesday happens to coincide with—Christmas, a major blizzard, torrential rainfall, or a heat wave—those in charge of each NADP station will do their utmost to collect the samples. C. L. Rawlins's book *Sky's Witness* provides an eloquent account of backcountry trips to collect NADP samples in the Wind River Range of Wyoming. My colleague Jill Baron of the US Geological Survey oversees the NADP sampling at Loch Vale, collecting the samples herself when her technicians are unable to make the trip for some reason (such as Christmas on a Tuesday). I have accompanied them on one of these autumn trips, driving up to the national park in the dark of very early morning, hiking along the frosty trail as the rising sun warmed us, then leaning into the winds at the Loch to collect the samples of stream and lake water.

Apparently, the only thing that can shut down the weekly sampling is the government. The September 2013 floods damaged every road leading into the eastern side of Rocky Mountain

Loch Vale in winter.

National Park, causing long detours for the weekly sampling trip. But the coup d'état to the sampling came during the shutdown of the federal government that followed the flood. All national parks around the country were closed, even to researchers. I was not along on the first trip during the shutdown, but Jill and her co-workers had climbed the long, steep trail up to Loch Vale before they were intercepted by law enforcement officers. Jill is a petite woman, but determined. During the ensuing discussion, handcuffs were mentioned. Things never reached that point, but the sampling was not completed. While politicians argued and postured in Washington, decades of continuous sampling were interrupted.

It is precisely because of such determination and dedication—passion—that we know that dust deposition has increased enormously in the Rocky Mountains. Why the increase? Probably multiple reasons. The southwestern United States has had long and severe droughts during the past twenty years. Drought decreases vegetation cover and soil moisture, allowing wind to more readily erode the soil. That appears to explain about half of the increase. The rest may reflect more disturbance of the soil from off-road vehicles, oil and gas development, and sprawl of urban and suburban areas as population increases across the Sun Belt.

The consequences of the increased dust deposition are equally diverse. The most solidly documented consequence is changes in snowmelt. As melting snow concentrates dust at the surface, the darker surface absorbs more solar energy and melts faster. The snowpack now melts up to a month earlier in the headwaters of the Colorado River basin on the western side of Rocky Mountain National Park, reducing runoff and water supplies by creating a shorter duration of snowmelt-fed stream flow. Some of the earlier melting reflects warming temperatures, but some reflects dust. One study of a relatively small mountain basin in the San Juan Mountains of southern Colorado found that snow cover disappeared from twenty-one to fifty-one days earlier in direct proportion to dust concentration on the snow surface. The effects across many small basins quickly add up. Cores of lake sediments from the eastern portion of the Upper Colorado River basin indicate that dust accumulation increased six-fold by the early twentieth century as a result of grazing, crops, and other land uses. The dust shortened the duration of snow cover by several weeks, causing peak river flow at Lees Ferry, Arizona—a flow gage on the Colorado River just upstream from the Grand Canyon—to occur on average three weeks earlier and decreasing annual runoff by more than 1 billion cubic yards, or about 5 percent of the annual average.

Thinking about these numbers, I remember the animated version of the Dr. Seuss story "Horton Hears a Who!" Horton is an elephant aware that a tiny dust speck contains a teeming world of miniature creatures. When Horton's fellow large creatures think he is crazy and taunt him with boiling the dust speck, the "Whos" all chant together, "We are here, we are here" until the bigger creatures hear them and stop short of boiling the Who-world. The billions of dust particles making vital water supplies vanish back into the atmosphere across the western United States might as well be shouting "We are here, we are here," but most of us have not yet begun to hear them even if we notice that late-season snowpacks seem to be dirty.

The less obvious consequences of increasing dust in the air involve human health. The occurrence in central Arizona of valley fever, a sometimes-fatal respiratory infection caused by wind-borne fungal spores, increased by almost ten times between 1998 and 2011. Asthma has also become increasingly common in parts of the rural western United States once known for good air quality.

The more subtle effects on park ecosystems of increased dust remain largely unknown. Aeolian dust can be an important source of carbon and other nutrients for alpine soils. As the snowpack melts in spring, carbon dust in the snowpack enters the soil, creating a boom in soil microbial populations. As microbial numbers decline later in the spring, nutrients become available for plants at the onset of the growing season. How these interactions among soils, microbes, and alpine vegetation will respond to more nutrients is an open question. Also unknown are the potential effects of the other materials blown in on the wind—pesticides, artificial fertilizers, heavy metals such as copper or cadmium, and industrial compounds.

The Glacier Creek watershed is one of the most scenic areas of the national park, from the view at the Storm Pass trailhead west to the peaks of the continental divide, to the backdrops of Bear Lake, Mills Lake, and Loch Vale. I can easily lose myself in the immediate details of my work here, but as I hike through and contemplate this superb scenery, I try to remember the invisible processes that underlie the geology, climate, and plant and animal communities creating the scenery. And with every staggering gust on this November day, I particularly remember that we all live downwind.

In this month of the year's shortest days, I turn to Bear Lake as
the iconic destination of Rocky Mountain National Park. The car
thermometer reads –6°F when I arrive at the Bear Lake parking
lot, although the sun has already cleared the horizon. The parking
lot is nearly empty and I am so eager to start that I am impatient
with the cold-stiff bindings of the snowshoes. Snow fell throughout
the day yesterday, silent and steady, and the sky at the base of the
mountains remains heavily overcast. But here in the park the sky
is radiantly, deeply, purely blue, the rich azure of lapis lazuli. This
is a day for adventuring and off I go, feeling a little foolish at first
on the well-packed trail at Bear Lake, but then quickly glad of the
snowshoes and poles as I begin to break trail in knee-deep powder.

Emerald Lake resembles one of Maxfield Parrish's paintings
in which the foreground is shadowed and the more distant view
is brightly lighted. Emerald Lake and its shorelines remain bluish
white in the deep shadows of a winter morning, but the snow-
covered cliffs to the west and south of the lake are so brilliantly
white that the sunlight seems to emanate from them.

The morning is silent but for the sounds I make: no wind, no
bird calls. Even the snow avalanches that occasionally cascade from
branches mounded under powder make only the softest shshshing
as they feather outward in falling through the air. Perhaps it is these
thousands of small snow collapses that fill the air with diamond
dust. When I look directly upward, even in a broad opening in the
forest, the air sparkles with millions of tiny ice crystals reflecting
the sunlight. Sunlight fills each opening, coming from above but
also from below and from every side, reflected by the infinite
mirrors of ice crystals on the ground, coating the trees and rocks,
and floating in the air. This is a diamond day of mostly stationary
ice crystals tossing the sunlight back and forth in a light show that
can feel almost blinding. Such winter days—when snow and sun

create the scenery and wind sits in the wings, waiting for its inevitable cue—are rare in the windy heights of Rocky Mountain National Park.

I keep moving, expecting the wind to wake up shortly and start rearranging the precariously poised tufts of snow that both accentuate and obscure every detail of the landscape. Miraculously, the air remains calm and only the gradually increasing warmth of the sun begins the process of rearrangement. More snow bombs start to drop from the trees, occasionally catching me beneath them in a bone-shuddering rush of chill. Clear ice appears at the edges of the spruce needles protruding below mounded snow, precursor of the tiny icicles that form later in the morning. Hoarfrost remains on the shadowed faces of boulders and dead trees, each crystal as intricately patterned as a feather or the frond of a fern. These are the ephemeral flowers of winter, gone as soon as sunlight reaches them or the air warms a little too much. Icicles rib the rock faces below joints. Where the icicles feed on water filtered by the rock, the ice is so clear that even in shadow the diffuse sunlight creates a pattern within the ice that changes as I move from side to side, as though the icicle contained its own fire. Icicles feeding on meltwater moving between snow and soil at the top of the rock form muddy brown streaks down the rock face. Snow, rock, and tree play with my sense of motion and fixity: snow crystals, transient as winter, rest in amorphous piles as though never to move again, while exposed beneath the piles are the twisted wood grain of trees and the contorted layers of rock, each seemingly caught momentarily in an ongoing forceful motion.

I flounder through thigh-deep powder where small avalanches have covered steep portions of the trail to Lake Haiyaha. More snow is moving down from the trees now and I begin to hear the birds. Chickadees call first: reliable, cheerful-sounding, winter-hardy. Then comes the knocking of a woodpecker echoing among the trees. A gray jay flutters in to land on a nearby branch, the usually vocal bird silent today but for the sound of its wings. The jay looks obese, with every feather on its body plumped out to maximize insulation against the killingly cold air. I see a few tracks in the newly fallen powder—the widely spaced leaps of a snowshoe hare or the more delicate imprints of a rodent landing lightly on the surface—but I know that even if the animals spent last night mostly sheltered from the quickly falling snow, they will be seeing about getting food now that the sun is once more bringing warmth.

I lose the trail partway along a steep slope. I feel reasonably sure that the trail switchbacks sharply and continues up the slope, but I can see no evidence of the track, so I continue straight for a few paces. I am quickly floundering, my right snowshoe plunging into a buried air pocket next to a downed tree. The snowshoe partly detaches from my boot and I have trouble pulling it back up to the surface and reattaching it firmly.

Buried cavities in the snow, whether created by obstacles under the snow or by burrowing animals, are critical to winter survival for many creatures. In his fascinating book *Winter World*, Bernd Heinrich describes ptarmigan and grouse burrowing into snow caves. He also writes of the subnivian zone at the base of the snowpack. Within the snowpack, temperatures are warmer close to the ground. This causes snow crystals to melt, creating water vapor that migrates upward, recondenses, and freezes onto the crystals of the upper snowpack. Over the course of the winter, the lower snowpack develops a subnivian zone analogous to an urban area, with ice pillars and columns forming the skyscrapers and extensive air spaces forming the streets and parks. Temperatures here remain within a degree or two of the freezing point of water, whatever the fluctuations in air temperature up above, thanks to the insulation of the snow and to heat rising from the ground. This subnivian world is the space in which mice, voles, and shrews spend the winter eating insects and the bark of trees and shrubs. The relative warmth of the subnivian also helps some early-blooming wildflowers like pasque flowers get an early start on their annual reproductive cycle.

I have seen the evidence of subnivian activities when melting of the snow in spring and early summer reveals sinuous mounds of sediment churned up by burrowing rodents and packed into subnivian tunnels by the meltwater flowing between the snowpack and the ground surface at the very end of snowmelt. The subnivian world is one of many reasons I am glad that snowmobiles are not allowed in Rocky Mountain National Park. The extensive swaths of compacted snow left across subalpine meadows by snowmobile rodeos in the adjacent national forest lands represent a few minutes' worth of fun that destroy critical winter habitat for an uncounted number of smaller creatures.

Back at Bear Lake, a short but cautious walk along the heavily trampled and icy snow mounds near the parking lot brings me to the edge of the lake. The lake is a flat, white plain closely surrounded by forest. Sunlight has raised the air temperature above 0°F in the clearings, but the air remains sharply cold in the shadows beneath the trees.

In this seasonal nadir of warmth, I admire the snowy scenery and think about climate warming. I believe that we have to understand the park's history—from the uplift of the Rockies tens of millions of years ago to the Pleistocene glaciers, the nineteenth-century miners and loggers, and twentieth-century nitrate deposition and water engineering—to understand the contemporary context and future trajectories that might occur in the park. One of the greatest unknowns of the future is how warming climate will change the park. The air will not just get warmer. A likely scenario is that climatic extremes, especially wet, dry, and hot, will become worse. The widespread, sustained rainfall of the September 2013 flood was outside the experience and expectations of anyone living in the region, including meteorologists. After the flood, many people asked, is this climate change? Some of the foremost climate scientists in the world live in Boulder, just east of Rocky Mountain National Park, and the consensus is that because a warming atmosphere holds more moisture, the big flood could be the face of climate change.

Certainly, warming climate will change the punctuated rhythms of climate that have existed for the past several thousand years since the Pleistocene glaciers melted. As climate goes, so goes the world: the rate at which bedrock weathers into sediment, and gravity, water, and ice move the sediment downslope; the types of plants and where they grow; the animals that feed on those plants or on other animals; the number, activity, and geographic range of mountain pine beetles and other insects that kill trees; the water available for people, the crops that can survive the new weather patterns and water availability; the fires that burn the forests and the structures that people build in those forests; and on and on.

I wonder how many of these changes I will actually perceive during my lifetime. I will be preoccupied with my own changing rhythms as I age. Those strenuous annual logjam surveys will not be feasible when I can no longer hike swiftly all day. With luck, I will take pleasure in memories of how I came to know this park from a hundred different entry points over more than a score of years.

For now, back down at Bear Lake, I watch the other visitors moving carefully along the icy trail around the lake. Bear Lake is the microcosm that reflects the diversity of Rocky Mountain National Park. Every park visitor wants to come here. The road to the lake is thick with traffic during summer and on autumn weekends. The lake itself, a scenic gem, is commonly enjoyed in the company of dozens, if not hundreds. But from the lake you can escape the crowds if you are willing to hike. The Flattop Mountain Trail ascends steadily to the continental divide and the paradox of the tundra, where the plants and many of the readily observed animals are diminutive but the world spreads to the expansive horizons. Other trails follow the canyons to the lakes less visited: Emerald, Dream, and Nymph; Haiyaha; Helene, Odessa, and Fern; Loch Vale, Lake of Glass, and Sky Pond; Mills and Black.

Each cascade of lakes has its own beauties and its own secrets. Steep walls of grayish tan granite horizontally seamed by lighter-colored intrusions tightly cup Emerald Lake. Trees and ground junipers lightly colonize the talus at the base of each rock wall and white threads of water in summer and ice in winter twist down from the summits. The talus records the slow crumbling of the rock, but this remains a landscape of rock, on which trees and water make only faint impressions here at the upper limits of their existence. I read the signs of past violence in the swirled intrusions of the rock walls and the wind-combed branches of the trees. Down-valley, Dream Lake occupies an obvious glacial trough where the trees, having more purchase, cover the north-facing slope. The giant, sharp-edged block of Hallett Peak at the northern head of the valley makes me think of how the landscape has been chopped out with a hatchet of ice. Farther down is Nymph Lake, safely cradled by trees, the peaks and their intense winds more distant. Here in summer water lilies bloom yellow in the greenish water.

At Haiyaha rocks emerge from the water at the southern edge, as though colonizing the lake, but the gray, green, and yellowish brown lichens covering the rocks reveal that the boulders moved long ago. The landscape of the lake is mostly quiet now, a rock foundation left to water and plants. In summer, dark stains on the cliff walls reveal water seeping from the seemingly impenetrable rock faces along vertical and horizontal seams where the bedrock leaks. These are the signs of rock falls to come.

Then there is Loch Vale, which I thought I knew reasonably well, until it revealed a whole new world to me one winter when I chanced to look more carefully down at the ice beneath my feet. Recorded there were the signs of life beneath the seemingly impenetrable lid of ice sealing the lake waters from air and sunlight. The ice held universes of tiny bubbles frozen into little streaks like

→

The next five photographs show different bubbles and cracks in the ice at Loch Vale.

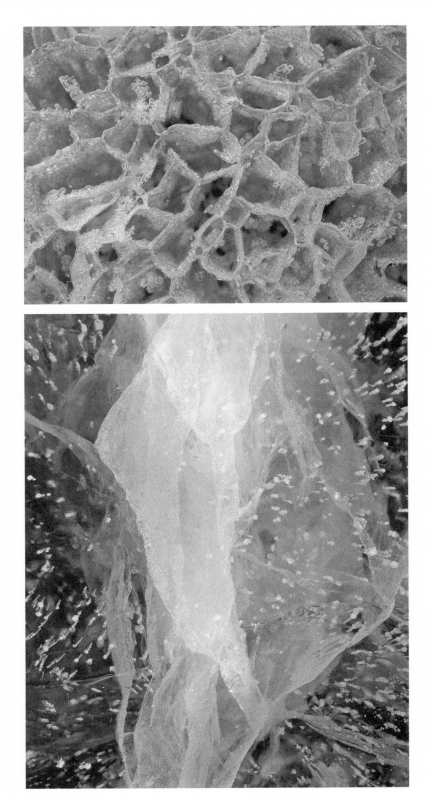

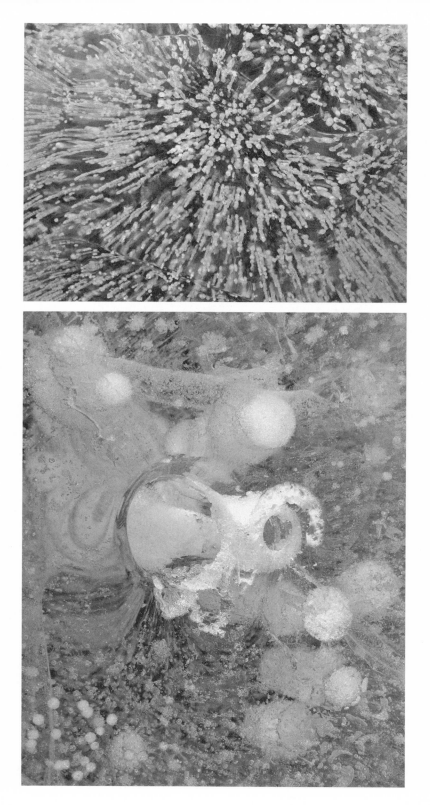

the tracks of stars moving apart after the Big Bang. Larger bubbles hung arrested in the act of swirling like whirlpools or expanding into a mushroom cloud. Cracks resembled the Milky Way and the honeycomb of a beehive.

A Personal Park

These are the names and memories that fill in the spaces on the park map. Among them lie the places on my mental map of the park, places that reveal the working of this ecosystem and changes in the landscape through time. At the Storm Pass trailhead near the Bierstadt Lake shuttle bus stop is a relatively small beaver meadow that has at least one active colony of beavers. Here I puzzled over what sort of red-colored fern could grow beneath the waters of a beaver pond until I realized that I was looking at the young shoot of an elephanthead—a plant that grows into a stalk of lovely magenta flowers, each of which resembles the head of an elephant. This beaver meadow was one of the sites where I collected sediment samples to measure how much carbon is stored in the floodplains

The view west to the high peaks from Storm Pass trailhead along Glacier Creek during summer. A small beaver meadow along the creek is in the foreground.

along different types of valley throughout the park. Active beaver meadows are filled with thick, black muck rich in carbon. These segments of the river network, although only a small portion of total river length, store a disproportionately large amount of the carbon present in the entire landscape. When beavers abandon a meadow, the sediments dry and some of the carbon is released to the atmosphere.

Beaver meadows and logjams frame my understanding of rivers, wilderness, and climate change in the park. As I contemplate the view from Bear Lake, I imagine individual jams tucked in for the winter beneath snow and ice. Just downstream from Alberta Falls was the huge jam that created a large backwater pool. In autumn, golden leaves fallen from the surrounding aspens floated on the dark water of the pool, collecting together and then drifting apart in a constantly changing mosaic. Then one year the jam vanished,

And early on a December morning.

dispersing down Glacier Creek all the rich muck accumulated in the pool, more than a hundred logs, and all the numbered aluminum tags I had laboriously nailed to the logs.

Upstream from Alberta Falls and Mills Lake is the big blowdown of 2011 that created new jams and a complicated pattern of branching channels that flow for 300 yards downstream before rejoining into a single channel. During the first summer, mature trees lay across Glacier Creek like blades of grass felled by the scythe of the wind. Their needles were still green. By the next summer, the branches of these fallen trees had collected other pieces of wood being carried down the creek, forming small logjams. The summer after that, many of the jams and the fallen trees had disappeared, swept away in the flood of September 2013. More trees fell, their roots undercut by stream banks eroded during the flood, or toppled by winter winds, and new jams were starting to form two summers after the flood. These I continue to watch.

And then there is the "Mother Ship," the jam on North St. Vrain Creek that I first studied in detail with my graduate students. We named it the Mother Ship because it was so large and solid that the intertwined logs and smaller branches created a formidable wall across the creek, backing water 50 yards up the channel in a deep pool carpeted with fine sand and fallen pine needles where fish resting in the eddies waited for an unwary insect to touch down on the water surface. We climbed all over that jam without fear of dislodging the logs or falling into the water. Then one year I noticed a breach in the wall: a suck of water against the right bank swirling downward as though entering the drain in a bathtub. By the next year, wood and sediment were clearly eroding at the widening breach and within two years the once-broad jam was reduced to a narrow, precarious bridge of logs underneath which the creek flowed freely. The pool drained and the fish moved elsewhere, but then another tree fell just upstream, began to catch smaller floating wood, and formed its own jam and backwater pool. This we christened the Daughter Ship.

Each year I finish my annual hikes down the creeks battered and bruised from scrambling through the downed wood away from trails, but intrigued by the changes I have seen since the previous year and happy with my feeling of gradually evolving understanding. Individual jams form and break apart, but as long as some remain present along the forested streams, each jam and its backwater pool create a hot spot where nutrients are stored, habitat is created, and insects and fish grow to abundance.

I enjoy watching the perceptions of my friends and colleagues change as they visit the sections of stream rich in logjams. Even those well versed in the importance of these features are taken aback at the apparent chaos of an old-growth area jumbled with downed wood. As one stream ecologist said on first seeing an old-growth patch along North St. Vrain Creek, "This place looks like a Tinker Toy factory exploded." With repeated visits, attitudes change from "Whoa, what happened here?" to "Ok, this is one end of the spectrum of 'normal.'"

Each of us judges the world based on our preconceptions and personal knowledge. My colleagues who study the chemistry of the Loch Vale ecosystem are concerned because they know that nitrates are accumulating in the soils and water. When I hike through the old-growth forest along North St. Vrain Creek early on a summer morning with newly hatched mayflies and rising mist backlit by the rising sun, all's right with the world. When I compare the abundance and diversity of the active beaver meadow at Wild Basin with the biologically poorer abandoned beaver sites now changed to dry grasslands in Moraine Park and Upper Beaver Meadows, all is not so right.

Paradoxes

As I stand at Bear Lake at the end of the year, I ponder the paradoxes of the park, a highly managed and relatively altered "wilderness" in which more than 3 million visitors a year trample heavily used sections of trail to dust and require bigger roads and campgrounds. I am continually tripped up by my own false expectations that the park will be a wilderness in which humans have had no part. I chide myself that these are Romantic fantasies. I remember one summer morning when I worked in Upper Beaver Meadows during the reconstruction of the Bear Lake Road. I was just thinking sourly that I might as well be down in a city with all the noise of the heavy equipment, when I saw five wild turkeys crossing the meadow. Then a coyote trotted by, pausing to cock its head sideways and listen to something moving in the grass before pouncing in a high arc on a small rodent. I walked into a stand of aspen at the edge of the valley and found an elk lying down, chewing placidly. Clearly, at least some of the local wildlife was not particularly perturbed by the construction noise.

Why does it matter so much if humans have altered this landscape? It matters because the history of alteration means that we are not starting from an intact ecosystem, complete with predators, for example, and we must therefore continue to actively intervene in the workings of this ecosystem. It matters because our property boundaries and land uses truncate ecosystems, migration routes, and habitat. Beavers, for example, may do better outside the national park, on adjacent national forest lands where elk are hunted. And it matters because we as a society cannot pat ourselves on the back and assume that we are finished because we have set aside a few natural areas in the national park system. We have managed to designate some less altered parcels of land, but there is no true wilderness in a time of human-induced climate warming. We cannot assume the luxury that there is some "away" or "apart," whether this is Rocky Mountain National Park or Alaska, because there no longer is.

I do not think this is cause for despair. Language matters: how we phrase and frame an issue or a question strongly influences how we think about responses or solutions to it. Are some of the changes in Rocky Mountain National Park during the past century human caused? Yes. Am I part of the cause? Yes. Is the response or solution beyond my influence? No. As one of my friends who is a climate scientist put it, we have an obesity problem in the United States. Do we blame calories? Do we blame farmers? Of course not. We put the blame on many other factors, including individual choices. We could apply the same reasoning to climate change, water engineering, atmospheric deposition, or extinction of species. These effects stem from many causes, including our individual choices.

My great-grandmother visited Rocky Mountain National Park as an elderly woman in 1930. I have a souvenir from that trip, a brochure issued by the Union Pacific System titled *Colorado Mountain Playgrounds*. I like to look at the black-and-white photographs of people in open touring cars driving between tall snow banks along Trail Ridge. One of the photos shows Bear Lake,

Photograph of Bear Lake in a 1930 Union Pacific railroad brochure. The large number of standing dead trees across the lake reflects the Bear Lake fire of 1900, which was started by an abandoned campfire.

which the caption describes as "sought because of its seclusion and primitive beauty." No one would describe Bear Lake as secluded today. The enormous parking lot quickly fills on summer mornings and those who don't rise with the sun can only reach the lake by shuttle bus. As beautiful as I find Bear Lake, this is why I seek the backcountry.

My research has provided an entrée into seldom-traveled portions of the park and that is without question one of the attractions of research for me. I enjoy the physical challenge of accessing remote streams and I appreciate my greater awareness of the surroundings when I work alone. Of equal importance, I am compelled by scientific questions about how rivers function under different conditions imposed by natural processes and by humans. These questions evolve with time as my understanding of the park environment changes. I have a history with sites visited year after year and this enhances my appreciation of the impact of episodic events such as the very high snowmelt flows of 2010 and 2011,

A view of Bear Lake during winter 2010 indicates regrowth of the forest after the fire.

the blowdowns during the winter of 2011–2012, or the drought of 2012. The logjams and beaver meadows to which I return each summer are my grains of sand in which I see the world.

Among the famous, heavily visited parks of the western United States—Yellowstone, Grand Canyon, Yosemite, Glacier—Rocky Mountain is relatively small and closely hemmed in by cities and agricultural lands. As I learn more about this national park, I find myself frequently mourning what has been lost: the extensive beaver meadows; pools with dozens of native trout; and wolves, grizzlies, wolverines, and bison. It is as though I see the ghosts of these animals when I come upon long-abandoned beaver dams far up a mountain stream or see the nineteenth-century photographs of men posing with dozens of cutthroat trout strung up behind them.

But even greater than the urge to mourn is the desire to

celebrate what remains. One of the qualities that makes this park special to me is its very proximity to my home. I live in an average suburban neighborhood in an average city, but in an hour I can be at a trailhead that is the portal to a place where humans do not necessarily dominate and where natural communities continue to surprise and enlighten. This is a central paradox of the park: it is so close to so many people that it is heavily used, yet its accessibility allows me to return repeatedly and come to know the landscape from different entry points through the seasons and the years. I love this park, and even though I am sometimes disappointed by what I learn of its history, love is not love which alters when it alteration finds. Rocky Mountain National Park remains the closest thing I know to the truth of this natural landscape.

This love and this sense of truth are what impel me to examine and question my individual choices and the choices of my society through a lens of what choices are best for the natural world. I do not have simple answers to the very difficult questions of how the national park service and concerned citizens can reduce problems starting outside the park boundaries or before the park was established, but I strongly believe that each of us must be aware of problems before we can know best what to do. My awareness leads me to embrace messiness—to revel in the physical complexity supported by beaver dams and logjams, as well as by blowdowns and wildfires—and to celebrate natives over introduced species. Awareness allows me to move beyond a view of the landscapes and ecosystems of the national park as static scenery and understand them as dynamic features continually changing over time periods short and long. I strive to see beyond obvious perceptions to the cryptic processes such as water moving down hillslopes to emerge in wet meadows perched above a stream, where my passage flushes songbirds nesting in the knee-high willow shrubs.

Sometimes this striving to see beyond the obvious is hard work. Despite my knowledge of natural extremes, Rocky Mountain National Park is not a place where I expect to directly experience natural disasters. I have worked in the Himalaya and been continually aware of the possibility of rock falls and landslides. And I have worked in the tropics and kept the proverbial one eye open for epiphyte-laden trees that come crashing down when even modest winds follow prolonged rain. But the park still strikes me as relatively benign. I hiked up to one of my remote sites on North St. Vrain Creek on Tuesday, September 10, 2013, the day before widespread flooding began. I had no inkling of what was occurring. Rain had fallen the day before and we had a chilly, damp day as moderate rain continued to fall steadily that Tuesday, but I never would have predicted that we were about to experience a major flood.

Scientists place a great deal of value on objectivity and are the first to criticize each other for not being objective. I could be the vaunted objective scientist and simply observe human alterations in the park while remaining emotionally detached, but this goes against my conscience. I am emotionally invested in this splendid place, not least because of my knowledge of some of its workings. (It's so cool, how can we stand to destroy it?) More than a decade ago, I attended a scientific workshop on reducing the effects of dams on river ecosystems. One scientist at the workshop lamented the increasing tendency of his colleagues to speak out about the damage done by dams to fish and river ecosystems. He traced this unfortunate tendency toward advocacy back to Rachel Carson. I left the workshop at the end of the day incensed and took a long walk in the woods surrounding the meeting place. Besides my deep admiration of Rachel Carson, his comments upset me because of my growing conviction that the special knowledge developed by scientists regarding the systems we study compels us to speak out. I have a responsibility to explain exactly what downed wood, and beavers, and physically complex rivers mean for biodiversity, water quality, and resilient ecosystems. I cannot dictate anyone else's behavior based on that knowledge, but I can work to ensure that our behavior does not result from ignorance of how we affect the world around us. There will likely always be people who do not care, no matter how much scientists strive to communicate their understanding of the complex and fascinating workings of natural systems. But my experience has been that many people do care and, if they are made aware of how human activities cause changes, prefer to cause fewer changes in national park ecosystems. We are all part of the problem and we are all part of the solution.

References

General

T.G. Andrews. 2015. Coyote Valley: deep history in the high Rockies. Harvard University Press, Cambridge, MA.

W. Bright. 2004. Colorado place names, 3rd ed. Johnson Books, Boulder, CO.

C.W. Buchholtz. 1983. Rocky Mountain National Park: a history. Colorado Associated University Press, Boulder, CO.

A. Drummond. 1995. Enos Mills: citizen of nature. University Press of Colorado, Boulder, CO.

J.J. Frank. 2013. Making Rocky Mountain National Park: the environmental history of an American treasure. University Press of Kansas, Lawrence, KS.

K. Hess. 1993. Rocky times in Rocky Mountain National Park: an unnatural history. University Press of Colorado, Niwot, CO.

E.A. Mills. 1915. The Rocky Mountain wonderland. Houghton Mifflin, Boston, MA.

R.W. Sellars. 1997. Preserving nature in the national parks: a history. Yale University Press, New Haven, CT.

E. Wohl. 2009. Of rock and rivers: seeking a sense of place in the American West. University of California Press, Berkeley, CA.

E.E. Wohl. 2001. Virtual rivers: lessons from the mountain rivers of the Colorado Front Range. Yale University Press, New Haven, CT.

W.A. Wyckoff. 1999. Creating Colorado: the making of a western American landscape, 1860–1940. Yale University Press, New Haven, CT.

M.T. Young. 2014. Rocky Mountain National Park: the first 100 years. Farcountry Press, Helena, MT.

A.H. Zwinger. 2002. Beyond the aspen grove. Johnson Books, Boulder, CO.

January

A.A. Borsa, D.C. Agnew, and D.R. Cayan. 2014. Ongoing drought-induced uplift in the western United States. Science, vol. 345, pp. 1587–1590.

February

T.G. Andrews. 2015. Coyote Valley: deep history in the high Rockies. Harvard University Press, Cambridge, MA.

S.L. Rathburn, Z.K. Rubin, and E. Wohl. 2013. Evaluating channel response to an extreme sedimentation event in the context of historical range of variability: Upper Colorado River, USA. Earth Surface Processes and Landforms, vol. 38, pp. 391–406.

Z.K. Rubin. 2010. Post-glacial valley evolution and post-disturbance channel response as a context for restoration, Upper Colorado River, Rocky Mountain National Park. MS thesis, Colorado State University, Fort Collins, CO, 143 pp.

Z. Rubin, S.L. Rathburn, E. Wohl, and D.L. Harry. 2012. Historic range of variability in geomorphic processes as a context for restoration: Rocky Mountain National Park, Colorado, USA. Earth Surface Processes and Landforms, vol. 37, pp. 209–222.

March

N. Kramer, E.E. Wohl, and D.L. Harry. 2012. Using ground penetrating radar to 'unearth' buried beaver dams. Geology, vol. 40, pp. 43–46.

April

E.A. Mills. 1913. In beaver world. Houghton Mifflin, Boston, MA.

W.D. Newmark. 1987. A land-bridge island perspective on mammalian extinctions in western North American parks. Nature, vol. 325, pp. 430–432.

W.D. Newmark. 1995. Extinction of mammal populations in western North American national parks. Conservation Biology, vol. 9, pp. 512–526.

D. Quammen. 1997. The song of the dodo: island biogeography in an age of extinction. Touchstone, New York, NY.

May

A.R. Dugmore. 1914. The romance of the beaver: being the history of the beaver in the western hemisphere. J.B. Lippincott, Philadelphia, PA.

L.E. Polvi and E. Wohl. 2012. The beaver-meadow complex revisited—the role of beavers in post-glacial floodplain development. Earth Surface Processes and Landforms, vol. 37, pp. 332–346.

L.E. Polvi and E. Wohl. 2013. Biotic drivers of stream planform: implications for understanding the past and restoring the future. BioScience, vol. 63, pp. 439–452.

C.J. Westbrook, D.J. Cooper, and B.W. Baker. 2006. Beaver dams and overbank floods influence groundwater-surface water interactions of a Rocky Mountain riparian area. Water Resources Research, vol. 42, W06404. doi:10.1029/2005WR004560.

C.J. Westbrook, D.J. Cooper, and B.W. Baker. 2011. Beaver assisted river
valley formation. River Research and Applications, vol. 27, pp. 247–256.

June
C.V. Baxter, K.D. Fausch, M. Murakami, and P.L. Chapman. 2004. Fish
invasion restructures stream and forest food webs by interrupting
reciprocal prey subsidies. Ecology, vol. 85, pp. 2656–2663.

J.R. Benjamin, F. Lepori, C.V. Baxter, and K.D. Fausch. 2013. Can
replacement of native by non-native trout alter stream-riparian food webs?
Freshwater Biology, vol. 58, pp. 1694–1709.

A.P. Covich, M.A. Palmer, and T.A. Crowl. 1999. The role of benthic
invertebrate species in freshwater ecosystems. BioScience, vol. 49, pp.
119–127.

N.L. Poff, J.D. Olden, D.M. Merritt, and D.M. Pepin. 2007. Homogenization
of regional river dynamics by dams and global biodiversity implications.
Proceedings of the National Academy of Sciences, vol. 104, pp. 5732–
5737.

D.W. Schindler and B.R. Parker. 2002. Biological pollutants: alien fishes in
mountain lakes. Water, Air, and Soil Pollution, vol. 2, pp. 379–397.

A.P. Wolfe, A.C. Van Gorp, and J.S. Baron. 2003. Recent ecological and
biogeochemical changes in alpine lakes of Rocky Mountain National
Park (Colorado, USA): a response to anthropogenic nitrogen deposition.
Geobiology, vol. 1, pp. 153–168.

July
E. Wohl. 2011. Threshold-induced complex behavior of wood in mountain
streams. Geology, vol. 39, pp. 587–590.

E. Wohl and N.D. Beckman. 2014. Leaky rivers: implications of the loss of
longitudinal fluvial disconnectivity in headwater streams. Geomorphology,
vol. 205, pp. 27–35.

E. Wohl and D. Cadol. 2011. Neighborhood matters: patterns and controls
on wood distribution in old-growth forest streams of the Colorado Front
Range, USA. Geomorphology, vol. 125, pp. 132–146.

August
K.B. Armitage, D.T. Blumstein, and B.C. Woods. 2003. Energetics of
hibernating yellow-bellied marmots (*Marmota flaviventris*). Comparative
Biochemistry and Physiology, Part A, vol. 134, pp. 101–114.

J.S. Baron, H.M. Rueth, A.M. Wolfe, K.R. Nydick, E.J. Allstott, J.T. Minear, and B. Moraska. 2000. Ecosystem responses to nitrogen deposition in the Colorado Front Range. Ecosystems, vol. 3, pp. 352–368.

D.J. Cooper. 2003. Beatrice E. Willard: In memoriam. Arctic, Antarctic, and Alpine Research, vol. 35, pp. 125–127.

M.E. Fenn, J.S. Baron, E.B. Allen, H.M. Rueth, K.R. Nydick, L. Geiser, W.D. Bowman, J.O. Sickman, T. Meixner, D.W. Johnson, and P. Neitlich. 2003. Ecological effects of nitrogen deposition in the western United States. BioScience, vol. 53, pp. 404–420.

D.H. Landers, A. Schwindt, K. Hageman, T. Blett, S. Simonich, S. Schreck, S. Usenko, M.M. Erway, D. Jaffe, M. Kent, L. Ackerman, L. Geiser, W. Hafner, J. Schrlau, D.H. Campbell, H.E. Taylor, and N. Rose. 2008. The fate, transport, and ecological impacts of airborne contaminants in western national parks (USA). Western Airborne Contaminants Assessment Project Final Report, volume 1. US Environmental Protection Agency, EPA/600/R-07/138, Washington, D.C.

J.W. Marr and B.E. Willard. 1970. Persisting vegetation in an alpine recreation area in the Southern Rocky Mountains, Colorado. Biological Conservation, vol. 2, pp. 97–104.

B.E. Willard and J.W. Marr. 1970. Effects of human activities on alpine tundra ecosystems in Rocky Mountain National Park, Colorado. Biological Conservation, vol. 2, pp. 257–265.

B.E. Willard and J.W. Marr. 1971. Recovery of alpine tundra under protection after damage by human activities in the Rocky Mountains of Colorado. Biological Conservation, vol. 3, pp. 181–190.

September

R.D. Jarrett and J.E. Costa. 1986. Hydrology, geomorphology, and dam-break modeling of the July 15, 1982 Lawn Lake Dam and Cascade Lake Dam failures, Larimer County, Colorado. U.S. Geological Survey Professional Paper 1369, Denver, Colorado.

J.F. McCain, L.R. Hoxit, R.A. Maddox, C.F. Chappell, F. Caracena, R.R. Shroba, P.W. Schmidt, E.J. Crosby, W.R. Hansen, and J.M. Soule. 1979. Storm and flood of July 31–August 1, 1976, in the Big Thompson River and Cache la Poudre River basins, Larimer and Weld Counties, Colorado. US Geological Survey Professional Paper 1115, Washington, DC.

P.C.D. Milly, J. Betancourt, M. Falkenmark, R.M. Hirsch, Z.W. Kundzewicz, D.P. Lettenmaier, and R.J. Stouffer. 2008. Stationarity is dead: whither water management? Science, vol. 319, pp. 573–574.

October

B.J. Bentz, J. Régnière, C.J. Fettig, E.M. Hansen, J.L. Hayes, J.A. Hicke, R.G. Kelsey, J.F. Negrón, and S.J. Seybold. 2010. Climate change and bark beetles of the western United States and Canada: direct and indirect effects. BioScience, vol. 60, pp. 602–613.

P.E. Dennison, S.C. Brewer, J.D. Arnold, and M.A. Moritz. 2014. Large wildfire trends in the western United States, 1984–2011. Geophysical Research Letters, vol. 41, pp. 2928–2933.

M.D. Flannigan, B.J. Stocks, and B.M. Wotton. 2000. Climate change and forest fires. The Science of the Total Environment, vol. 262, pp. 221–229.

J.A. Hicke, M.C. Johnson, J.L. Hayes, and H.K. Preisler. 2012. Effects of bark beetle-caused mortality on wildfire. Forest Ecology and Management, vol. 271, pp. 81–90.

J.A. Hicke, J.A. Logan, J. Powell, and D.S. Ojima. 2006. Changing temperatures influence suitability for modeled mountain pine beetle (*Dendroctonus ponderosae*) outbreaks in the western United States. Journal of Geophysical Research, vol. 111, G02019.

J.S. Littell, D. McKenzie, D.L. Peterson, and A.L. Westerling. 2009. Climate and wildfire area burned in western US ecoprovinces, 1916–2003. Ecological Applications, vol. 19, pp. 1003–1021.

S.J. Pyne. 1982. Fire in America: a cultural history of wildland and rural fire. Princeton University Press, Princeton, NJ.

T.T. Veblen and J.A. Donnegan. 2005. Historical range of variability for forest vegetation of the national forests of the Colorado Front Range. Final report, USDA Forest Service Agreement No. 1102-0001-99-033, Boulder, Colorado.

A.L. Westerling, H.G. Hidalgo, D.E. Cayan, and T.W. Swetnam. 2006. Warming and earlier spring increase western U.S. forest wildfire activity. Science, vol. 313, pp. 940–943.

November

J. Brahney, A.P. Ballantyne, C. Sievers, and J.C. Neff. 2013. Increasing Ca^{2+} deposition in the western US: the role of mineral aerosols. Aeolian Research, vol. 10, pp. 77–87.

J.M. Byrne, A. Berg, and I. Townshen. 1999. Linking observed and general circulation model upper air circulation patterns and future snow runoff for the Rocky Mountains. Water Resources Research, vol. 35, pp. 3793–3802.

C. Derksen and R. Brown. 2012. Spring snow cover extent reductions in the

2008–2012 period exceeding climate model projections. Geophysical Research Letters, vol. 39, L19504.

R.E. Ley, M.W. Williams, and S.K. Schmidt. 2004. Microbial population dynamics in an extreme environment: controlling factors in talus soils at 3750 m in the Colorado Rocky Mountains. Biogeochemistry, vol. 68, pp. 313–335.

N. Mladenov, M.W. Williams, S.K. Schmidt, and K. Cawley. 2012. Atmospheric deposition as a source of carbon and nutrients to an alpine catchment of the Colorado Rocky Mountains. Biogeosciences, vol. 9, pp. 3337–3355.

P.W. Mote, A.F. Hamlet, M.P. Clark, and D.P. Lettenmaier. 2005. Declining mountain snowpack in western North America. Bulletin of the American Meteorological Society, vol. 86, pp. 39–49.

T.H. Painter, J.S. Deems, J. Belnap, A.F. Hamlet, C.C. Landry, and B. Udall. 2014. Response of Colorado River runoff to dust radiative forcing in snow. Proceedings of the National Academy of Sciences.

S.B. Rood, J. Pan, K.M. Gill, C.G. Franks, G.M. Samuelson, and A. Shepherd. 2008. Declining summer flows of Rocky Mountain rivers: changing seasonal hydrology and probable impacts on floodplain forests. Journal of Hydrology, vol. 349, pp. 397–410.

S.M. Skiles, T.H. Painter, J.S. Deems, A.C. Bryant, and C.C. Landry. 2012. Dust radiative forcing in snow of the Upper Colorado River Basin: 2. Interannual variability in radiative forcing and snowmelt rates. Water Resources Research, vol. 48, W07522.

I.T. Stewart, D.R. Cayan, and M.D. Dettinger. 2005. Changes toward earlier streamflow timing across western North America. Journal of Climate, vol. 18, pp. 1136–1155.

P.J. Von Mantgem, N.L. Stephenson, J.C. Byrne, L.D. Daniels, J.F. Franklin, P.Z. Fule, M.E. Harmon, A.J. Larson, J.M. Smith, A.H. Taylor, and T.T. Veblen. 2009. Widespread increase in tree mortality rates in the western United States. Science, vol. 323, pp. 521–524.

E. Wohl. 2013. Redistribution of forest carbon caused by patch blowdowns in subalpine forests of the Southern Rocky Mountains, USA. Global Biogeochemical Cycles, vol. 27, pp. 1205–1213.

December

B. Heinrich. 2003. Winter world: the ingenuity of animal survival. HarperCollins, New York.

Index

Lawn Lake, 100, 141–143. *See also* Fall
River
leaky rivers, 119–123
Lily Lake, 57–60, 65–71, 73, 75
Loch Vale, 108 (photo), 185 (photo),
194
bubbles in ice of, 194–197
glacial history of, 93, 95–96
logjams, 72–73, 92, 115 (photo),
123, 170, 177, 199–201
nitrogen in, 108, 185–186
and stream ecology, 22–23, 113–122
and trout, 114
Longs Peak, 13, 58, 60, 66, 68 (photo),
111, 142
Lulu City, 27, 32–33, 164. *See also*
mining
luminescence dating, 51–52, 53

marmot, 73, 98, 128 (photo), 129, 139,
146
Merriam, C. Hart, 60–61
microburst, 20, 178. *See also* blowdown
Milankovitch, Milutin, 12, 95
Mill Creek, 164–165, 176
Mills, Enos, 65–66, 73
Mills Lake, 93, 108, 183, 185, 188, 193,
199, color photo 13
mining, 6, 29–30, 164. *See also* Lulu City
Mission 66, 137–138
montane vegetation zone, 16–17, 20,
163, 179, 182
moose, 24, 28–29, 39, 49–50, 75, 79, 81,
83, 84, 86, 170, 171 (photo)
moraine, 46–48, 56, 80, 142
Moraine Park, x, 41, 42 (photo), 45–48,
50, 53–57, 135, color photo 3
mountain pine beetle, x, 7, 22–23, 38,
161–162, 168, 173, 179–182, 193

National Atmospheric Deposition
Program (NADP), 184–185. *See
also* dust, aeolian

National Park Service, 133
and resource management, 32, 35,
38, 54–55, 57, 72, 75, 91, 100,
102, 131, 135, 137–138, 166, 182
Native American, 8, 163. *See also*
Arapaho; Ute
Never Summer Mountains, 29
nitrate, 38, 115, 184, 192, 201
nitrogen, 1, 4, 22, 82, 104, 106–109, 113,
114, 121, 123, 132–135, 139, 150
North St. Vrain Creek, 67 (photo), 84
(photo)
logjams, 200–201
watershed, 9–10, 72–73, 176
nutrients, 88, 104, 106–107, 113, 117,
168
and rivers, 23, 82, 105, 113–114,
121–123, 141, 150, 170–171,
200
and soils, 132, 188
and wildfire, 160

old-growth forest, 17, 20, 22, 96, 112,
116, 119–121, 160, 180, 182, 200
organic matter in rivers, 23, 82, 115
orogeny, 126–127
ouzel, 22, 63, 97, 106, 116, 178
Ouzel Creek, 9, 93, 166–167
Ouzel Falls, 10, 24, color photo 1
Ouzel Lake, 93

PCBs, 134–135
pesticides, 134–135, 188
pikas, 58, 63, 68, 98, 128, 130–131, 130
(photo), 137, 146
Pleistocene, 10, 45–48, 80, 182
pluton, 126–127
Poudre River, 27, 31, 72, 80
precession of Earth's orbit, 12
prior appropriation, 30–31
ptarmigan, 128, 129, 191, 219

Quaternary, 51–53

radiocarbon age, 36, 94
radiocarbon dating, 51–52, 94
Rathbun, Sara, 33–36, 41, 110–112, 115–118, 115 (photo), 123
restoration
    riparian, 91
    river, 44, 156, 170
riparian, 91, 121, 136, 150, 178
    doctrine, 30
Roaring River, 142–143, 146–147

Sandbeach Creek, 9, 23
Sandbeach Lake, 99
Sibold, Jason, 97, 169
Snowmass, 45, 47
South Platte River, 13, 29, 31, 72, 84
stationarity, 155
St. Vrain, Ceran, 83–84
subalpine, 113, 163, 173–174, 176, 179
    lake, 5
    vegetation zone, 16, 19–20, 159, 179–182

talus, 9, 93, 194
tectonic plate, 56, 125–127
tilt of Earth's axis, 10–12
Tonahutu Creek, 136, 158, 160, 163, 169–170, color photo 12
Trail Ridge Road, vii, 25, 110, 136–138

trout
    brook, 102, 104–105
    brown, 102
    cutthroat, 100, 101, 103–105, 118, 120
    rainbow, 102–104
    See also greenback cutthroat trout
tularemia, 68–69
tundra, 20–21, 21 (photo), 58, 129–130, 137–139. See also alpine: vegetation zone

Ute, 163, 169. See also Arapaho; Native American

water table, 50, 88
Wild Basin, 7–9, 19, 25, 67, 75, 81, 201
wildfire, 3, 4, 17–18, 21, 54–55, 97, 147, 158–169, 167 (photo), 179–180, 203 (photo), color photo 15
    Big Meadows, 157
    Fern Lake, 97, 157, 167
    recurrence intervals, 17, 19, 159
Willard, Beatrice, 137–138
Wilson, E. O., 53, 69
wolf, 38, 64, 65, 86–87, 204

Yellowstone, 27, 65, 70, 137, 166, 204
    and beavers, 87–88, 90